Shooter in the Sky

Shooter
in the Sky

The Inner World of
Children Who Kill

Dr. Lauren J. Woodhouse

CORINTHIAN
BOOKS

Mount Pleasant, S. C.

Cataloguing-in-Publication
(Provided by Quality Books, Inc.)

Woodhouse, Lauren J.
    Shooter in the sky: The inner world of children who kill /
    Dr. Lauren J. Woodhouse — 1st ed.
    p. cm.
    Includes bibliographical references (p.)
    LCN 00-106584
    ISBN 1-929175-02-7 (hc)
    ISBN 1-929175-13-2 (sc)

    1. Juvenile homicide—United States.   2. Homicide—United States—Psychological aspects.   I. Title

HV6529.W66 2001   364.15'23'0973
                                    QBI00-901204

Corinthian Books
an imprint of
the Côté Literary Group
P. O. Box 1898
Mt. Pleasant, S. C. 29465-1898
(843) 881-6080
http://www.corinthianbooks.com

Contents

Acknowledgments

I WOULD LIKE TO THANK several boys for sharing their feelings about having committed seriously violent acts, and for further sharing their experiences, terrors, inner journeys, and growth in the wake of the widespread destruction of lives, including their own. I also benefited enormously from discussions with and written work by over a hundred adolescents who spoke to me about their fears, insecurities, isolation, sense of hopelessness, and, in many cases, their inclinations toward violence. I would also like to thank the "leaders" of three street and two school gangs for allowing me to get to know them, their friends, and their shared perspectives.

I need to thank two county sheriffs, both of whom asked that their names not be mentioned, but who took the time to speak with me at length, and earnestly, about their jobs during and in the aftermath of children killing children.

I also want to acknowledge each and every teacher heroically manning the fort at public schools across North America. They take the heat from all sides with little compensation or protection. They are heroes, albeit tired ones, and many of them spoke to me of the bitterness that comes with lost idealism and the necessary closing of once open hearts. We understand, and we hope that they and their school boards will have the courage and wisdom to face the issue of violence from and among children head-on – partly through vehicles such as this book. Sections of it are unavoidably unpleasant by necessity. However, teachers and students know best that there is little room for perfunctory niceties when dealing with a truth as brutal and sad as children murdering children.

I further thank members of various police forces and the many parents who spoke with me about their direct and indirect experiences with lost and violent youth.

Foreword

Aₛ A SENIOR PSYCHIATRIST, mother, and grandmother, I am not sure that it is possible to describe the uncanny depth of understanding and the peculiar genius required to have written this gut-wrenching, accurate story about a young boy becoming sufficiently lost in the day-to-day of growing up to evolve into a murderer. In spite of having known Dr. Woodhouse for a number of years, and being aware of her hands-on work with and devotion to troubled youth, I am nevertheless astounded by the stinging realism captured in these pages. We come to know this boy, whom she calls Harold Connally, as he tells us his story, and, regardless of what he has done, we come to care about what happens to him. We also come to understand how he became lost, and develop a discomfiting urge to shield him as he realizes and confronts the full consequences of his actions.

Dr. Woodhouse has spent countless hours with youth, parents, and entire communities for whom reality was changed overnight and forever by a child homicide. She has come as close as possible to the hearts, inner worlds, and nightmares of tormented young souls. Perhaps this is why the boy in this story speaks to us in such a way so as to become painfully close to *our* hearts, virtually our child, but already beyond our ability to pull him back to safety.

When the author responds in interviews about this book, she deflects the awe implicit in questions about her having worn the psyche and shared the heartbeat of a teenage boy who kills. It is precisely this persistently courageous descent into the underworld of teen madness that makes this story so astoundingly accurate and riveting. Indeed, the immeasurable usefulness of this book aside, Lauren Woodhouse has met J. D. Salinger where he left off with *Catcher in the Rye*. This work will no doubt be as controversial in this time as Salinger's was in his. Salinger was daringly honest when he wrote about the doubts, insecurities, fears, and secrets of a solitary teenage boy in a much less complex world. He was true to his character – to reality – by not censoring and thereby aligning scenes, sentences, phrases, and language with popular, comfortably camouflaging sensibilities.

Likewise, Lauren Woodhouse has displayed the same courage and persistent loyalty to her teenage sources, the raw, accurate expression of their emotions and concerns, and to her work. What she is determined to have us learn and understand is more harrowing than Salinger's brilliant depictions of his young man's academic, sexual, and social frustrations, and self-vitiating loneliness. Dr. Woodhouse has *had* to go further – frighteningly further. In Salinger's day, the controversial issue was masturbation. Now, it's murder – and sometimes, mass murder, as at Columbine High School and increasingly more places.

Parents, teachers, social workers, and teenagers will benefit from reading and openly discussing a story about what is commonly dismissed as a random horrible, irrational act. I cannot imagine anyone starting to read this book, joining the tragic protagonist in the first chapter, and ever having him leave his or her heart.

In spite of having seen and treated the worst of madness on two continents over many years, and having reached a time in my professional and personal life when I am no longer easily impressed, excited, or drawn to new commitments, I am honored to be a part of this step forward in truth. I consider it a privilege to both know this determined practitioner and talented author, as well as to join her in what will no doubt be a groundbreaking, transformational book, which will trigger a fundamental paradigm shift in how we view troubled adolescents.

—Dr. Linda A. Morse
Psychiatrist and Psychoanalyst

Preface

T HIS BOOK IS A FICTIONALIZED COMPOSITE biography
of a child who kills. It may not be easy to read — nor should it
be. The despair, fear, anguish, confusion and nightmarish bru-
tality experienced by the boys I interviewed are all real,
discomfortingly communicated through this one boy's story.
However, there is a purpose for telling this story and accu-
rately communicating the horrors experienced by a child who
kills. The thinking and complex emotional world of a child
before and after resorting to murder is the what, how, and *why*
of this book.

Based on innumerable interviews with troubled children
and teens, as well as with adolescents who have resorted to
violence, this story illuminates a dichotomy that is often hard
to accept. That is, on the one hand, so-called "normal" children can suddenly lash out violently, even murderously, at us
and each other, and the other is that their drastic actions *can*
be understood and prevented — but frequently are not.

The way in which one reads, processes and uses this work
is critical to the objective of enabling readers – especially adolescents – to acquire a better understanding of themselves, and
of why seemingly "normal" children kill. The best way to do

this is to make use of the questions formulated for each chapter. The questions can also be used by parents and teachers to induce open discussions about the feelings and the thinking of both average and troubled teens.

As indicated in the body of research alluded to in my previous book, *Hard Lessons: Understanding and Addressing the Dangerous Challenges Facing Today's Youth*, our children are more fearful of being hurt, stabbed, or shot at school than we parents are for them. They don't talk about it, and they need us to give them a ready opportunity to do so. This book serves this purpose. This boy's story is sufficiently authentic to capture and maintain the interest a child in his early to late teens. By censoring typical adolescent language and imagery as little as possible, the book tells the truth, and, therefore, can honestly and effectively capture the attention to address the hearts and minds of confused teenagers. This visceral language – well-known to children – may offend some parents, but sugar-coating the pill is not a solution for the problem of child violence. Until now, none of us has had much to work with other than potentially inciting news broadcasts and worn platitudes and frowns from vocal, if ill-attuned, adults. As a result, we, too, have been flailing with decreasing credibility and an increasing sense of estrangement and helplessness ourselves.

In addition to increasing our understanding of the inner world of adolescents who end up in serious trouble, *Shooter in the Sky* is a virtual textbook on *consequences*. In discussions on child violence, it is critical that we depict what really happens to the life of a child, from one day to the next, when he makes the decision – or resigns himself to – killing as a form of self-assertion or mollification. Until now, this has been largely sidestepped in order to avoid offending "nice" families.

It is time to face this social issue head on, with words and with tears – both in our schools and at home. Merely reacting is no longer acceptable. I have presented a solid blue-print from which to start intelligent and preventive discussions. It is also a story and lesson through which we can attempt to reach and to touch the hearts of a generation left to simmer without clear ethical or behavioral guidelines. In short, we should, after reading and working with this story and model, be more alert and attentive to those among our children who are most likely to commit random acts of violence.

— Lauren J. Woodhouse, D.Psy., Ph.D. D.Div.

To G. and W., wishing you had lived, and knowing you would have joined my weak attempt to try to make the world a more comprehensible, gentler place. While I will always miss you, you live on in my heart and often bring light to the dark ache of loss. To Robert Taylor, who recently left us after a life of rich contribution, and to Liam for the same old reasons. To Luke, Kyle, and Jake, my dear nephews, who both delight me and alight my heart. I know that you will grow to be strong and secure in your own skin. Also, and again, to Helen Carenza Conte, the mother I never knew, and won't, but whose posture toward me has made me stronger, more determined, accomplished, and uncannily empathetic toward the lonely, disenfranchised, and abandoned. And, indeed, to mothers and parents everywhere who chose more courageous and loving alternatives. Our children owe you much.

ONE

Died Down

I DON'T KNOW IF this is what you want. I mean, you didn't give me much to go on, so I'm just blathering into this little tape recorder you left with a thousand little tapes and I don't know what's important, so I'm just telling you what I can think of or remember.

You said to talk about how I got here (and I'm smart enough to know that you *didn't* mean in a police car). I'm trying to find a place to start that makes sense, but I end up going all over the place and all that.

How can I tell whether you will listen to this anyway? Maybe I should put in some trick questions that you have to answer to see if you fast-forwarded or something because I got too boring.

Yeah, if you ever come back, I'll ask you stuff and see if I'm just wasting my time. I just made a joke. I guess it's a prison joke.

Wasting my time.

That's the joke, in case you didn't get it. I don't have normal time anymore and there aren't many things I have to rush to do here. I know it will change when I get moved to juvenile and all because they'll want to teach me some skills and make me earn my keep, as my dad would say.

I'm just waiting. It seems all I do is wait. I don't even know how long I've been here because I didn't start to wait, or even notice time at all, until last night.

It was like I had been away somewhere and then after, I forgot where I was. I sort of remember doing the thing, but not anything since the assholes brought me here and called me a piece of shit and all kinds of gross things. I remember a bit more now. I remember that after they shut up about the mess I caused, they put me where I am now and I sat on the floor, pressing my back into the metal side of this stupid cot. Now my back hurts as if someone hit me with a pipe or something.

By last night, my legs and knees were shaking, and no matter what I did, I couldn't keep them together. I even wrapped my arms real tight around them and put my head down to make myself into a ball, but the stupid things kept trembling and pulling apart like a wishbone. You know that weird bone on a turkey that everyone wants to play a game with at Thanksgiving and all? They make a wish, rip it apart and laugh because some idiot gets more of the dead thing's bone than someone else. It's just really stupid, if you ask me. All these nice parents who've got kids and tell them to be nice and then get their kicks ripping bones apart. Sick bastards.

I know I'm in what they call the holding center. I know that because I remember when they pretended to chase me to make it sound better for them later and they grabbed me. I punched one of the meaner cops in the nose and he radioed that he was, "taking the little bastard into holding."

Another cop had to pull him off me because he looked like he was going to kill me. He already had me down on the ground with his huge fists sort of bouncing me around and his sausage fingers were gouging into my ears and mouth. He even pushed my left eye in so hard, I remember thinking I might end up with a hole there and get to wear a patch. I know he was partly doing it to show me that he could easily toss me across the schoolyard or kill me in some other super-macho way if he wanted to.

But who was arguing? I'm not stupid. At least I don't think I am. Then another cop pushed me into their special car with no handles in the backseat and a steel, crisscross barricade between them and me. I've seen them put police dogs there before. I forgot that it was really a car cage for people.

Guess it makes sense, even though I sure wasn't going to climb over the seat to try to strangle them or anything. I was tired, but I also knew the blond one who wanted to kill me would shoot my head off if I dared to talk. I didn't even dare breathe too loud.

They were taking me to the station. That's where the holding center was. They said that on the police radio too, which I thought was really cool to listen to, especially when everyone's all tensed up and taking things seriously. I heard the nicer cop, who didn't have to prove he could kill me, say that he was taking me ". . .straight to the center."

It sounded sort of weird, like when my mother would say, "Straight to your room!" and for about five years now I've just laughed and ignored her. What's she going to do? Plus, I spend most of my time in my room anyway – it's my place and all. It's like ordering me "straight to the only place I feel comfortable! Right now!" Oh, okay.

When they brought me in, all cuffed and everything, I kept my head down, but everyone, even old cops, looking like they should be retired and should've seen *everything* by now, kept staring at me and stretching their necks to get a better look. I wish I weren't so normal — no — *sub*normal looking. They didn't look too impressed once they got a good look. They just seemed sort of disappointed, but disgusted at the same time.

Another cop came over and three big cops followed him. They took me into a back room, pressed my fingers into an ink pad until it was all over my fingers and hands, and took my picture a few hundred times.

I hate pictures. I told them I hate having my picture taken. Why does everyone laugh when you tell them that, and then just take your picture anyway? Why is that?

My whole life I'd say, "*Don't*," and try to get away, but everyone'd just laugh as if it was a big joke and do it anyway. At the jail, though, I didn't tell them to stop. The cops just kept on taking pictures — front, side, back, all the time mocking me about my name. It was hanging above a number around my neck. So it was bound to be used against me, as usual. Nothing new, but this time I couldn't fight back or leave.

"Turn this way, Harold," "Turn around Crazy Connally," "Hey, Harold, you related to Pee Wee? You a killer and a faggot too? Are you, Haarrold?"

After they had taken about a million pictures, they made me strip, all the while calling me names and then telling me I had a dick like a broken crayon. It was just like in gym class when I'd tried to hide it in the shower. Someone would rip my towel off or hotshots would drag me out and everyone would laugh at my dick. It's pretty small to be sure, and I'm not too happy about that, but I hated *that* much more than having my picture taken.

One cop even said my parents must have known I was a faggot at birth and so they gave me a faggot name – a name that could be turned into "Harriot" if I didn't grow a real dick. Luckily, I was out of it, sort of spaced, or I might've cried. I would've hated that. I don't ever remember crying even though my mother used to say I cried a lot when I was a toddler (which sounds like a baby toad to me!). All I know is I was extra weird, sort of weaker, around my father.

I thought my dad was God or something and I remember wanting to be around him until I got the message that he didn't like me. I hadn't earned his respect or something, so I stayed away from him. I mean, he wasn't impressed by crayon drawings and building blocks. I was just kind of in his way.

My mom caught on before I did and tried to keep me out of his path, not because he'd punch me out or anything, but because I might be "under foot" and irritate him if I was in the same room. *Under foot* — I always took that as a warning. If I didn't split, I'd be squished under his massive shoes and weight.

I rapidly learned to be absent even though I was there, you know what I mean? I existed, but I didn't at the same time, so that he could have what he always called "peace in his own home." The rest of us, especially me, just had to be careful. We, my sister and I, were told pretty early not to bug him.

After covering me with ink and taking ugly photographs, they checked my ass. They went right up in there with their hands covered with gloves, two of them, one after another, as if I might have grenades up there or something. When I sort of twisted when they were in there, they called me a wimp and went in deeper and poked around harder. I thought I was going to shit on them, like I couldn't help it, and even though I would've liked to just to gross them out, I didn't want to give them more reason to mock me, so I tried to hold it.

Even now when I move, as I'm remembering, my ass hurts like hell. When they were finished, they gave me this gross green top and matching baggy pants about a thousand sizes too big that I'm wearing now.

Then, they put me in this little cement room with nothing in it but a hard cot and a stained toilet with no seat. There isn't even a sink. One guy laughed at me through the bars, told me that I could help myself to the can if I got thirsty.

I did mess my pants at some point — probably that night because of what they did. *They're* the homos. I'm just thirteen and they were going at my butt the way my uncle, who owns a farm, sticks his whole arm into a cow to deliver a calf!

They also pulled my arm so hard it came out of my shoulder. I didn't feel it right away, just like the other big thing, the thing I did, I didn't quite remember, or have thoughts or anything about it. It feels as if my side is on fire right now, especially if I move. Luckily, I don't have to unless they come back to check me out again. If they ever try that again, I'll fart in their fat, sweaty faces and laugh at them. I won't say anything, though. I couldn't talk then and I am not sure I can now. I won't try anyway.

I often can't talk. I mean way before this happened. Maybe, if I'm lucky, I'll never talk again. What's the point? As my father would say, I've "cooked my goose," "made my bed." I didn't even yell when the guy pulled my arm and I saw it hanging wrong.

Just like with my dad, I didn't yell. I never shouted or cried when I knew he wanted me to. He'd get mad because I wasn't good at something and then laugh at me and introduce me to his friends as his youngest "daughter," as if it was the funniest thing in the whole world.

Everyone would just act embarrassed when he said it. Otherwise, he just called me shithead or worse, or would say things like, "Where the hell are your brains?!" Answering himself, he'd swear and say, "You don't have a brain to mess with!" It drove him crazy that I didn't look hurt or angry. He'd say, "Don't you even care what others think of you?! Don't you want to be a man and make something of yourself?!" I'd just listen until he told me to get out of his face.

These guys here are sort of the same. They wanted me to cry or scream or something, but even after I punched the guy, I didn't make any noise or move except when they pushed me. People like you to react to them the way they think you should or because they're so messed up that they need you to.

My dad did it with my mom. My mom always had the same reaction when he got angry: she'd do laundry, dishes, or wash the floor with a sick look on her face. My dad would just walk around the house, sometimes go outside, and keep coming in to check on her to make sure she still looked sad. Otherwise, he'd go at her again.

It was pathetic. She always gave him the reaction he wanted, like she was some kind of remote control wife or something. Even though he could pretend to be pretty cool sometimes, he was such a jerk with her. I don't care much about me, especially now that I don't even have to try anymore, but he always seemed to make her look sad.

Thinking of it makes me want to puke. I never *ever* want to react the way people want me to. I'd rather die, better still, be *killed* by someone who was trying to make me scream, talk back, or cry, so that they could feel bigger and more powerful. Some people act as if they have more rights than me. That's the kind of crap that really gets to me. Always has.

Teachers can be worse. They're losers. The only way they can feel as if they're a "somebody" is by bossing kids around. Big deal! What's worse, the asshole kids who let them are cop-outs, sucks and ass-lickers. I'd never give head for a mark in school or to get a stupid, blackmailing teacher to like me and then pass me even though I failed. I'd kill before I'd give head. I really would. I guess I did, but not for that. I can't talk or think about that yet. Mostly, because I don't feel anything. I just feel sort of relieved. So, I must not be able to really think about it yet or I might feel something, but not know it.

I'm too tense to sleep. I paced a bit a half hour ago, but mostly I just want to squat here against this stinky excuse for a bed. It's like the bed I had at camp last summer as a counselor in training to take care of little kids, except that it's older and smells like piss and B.O. A million guys probably jacked off on it.

When I got up off the floor, it was partly to get away from the stench. I did circles and then reverse circles within about eight square feet of dirty cement with *Fuck You* scratched into it in about a thousand places. Direction doesn't matter.

No matter which way I went, it led back to the stench of the cot, my sore ass and more *Fuck Yous*. Kind of symbolic, you might say, but I didn't say it on purpose. I'm not that smart and I'm not clear enough about anything to be smart about anything specific either.

I'm just waiting, as always, but in a different way. In a way, this waiting is safer. I prefer to not know what I'm waiting for, if that makes any sense at all. Some other guys have brought me food and water and stuff, but I don't feel like eating. I don't feel anything, especially hunger. I almost feel full, as if I'll never need to eat again – same with sleep.

Another doctor – a normal one, not a head-shrinker – came in and gave me a pill before they sent you. All *you* did was walk in, ask how I felt, as if I should be feeling great or something, and told me to talk into this spiffy little sneaky shrink's tape recorder. Then you said, "Take care," like I could, and left.

All *he* said was, "Take this and sleep," like a robo-doc. He didn't give a damn. He was just doing his job like you, like Mr. Tarkin, the principal of my school. He was just doing his job by kicking me out and making my dad want to get me into therapy again, and make me cry and beg for another chance. That's how this sort of started.

Tarkin hurt my mom too because she's always been worried about me. I always hated that. I always wondered what was so wrong with me that made her so worried. Tarkin made her worry more and caused my dad to go at her again. All night he yelled and told her it was her fault I was useless. She started to clean everything in sight, even the ceilings, just taking it and taking it, as usual.

In the past, when my dad pulled this kind of stuff, he'd tell me a few days later that he was just doing his job as a parent. He was "guiding" me so that I would have a "future." He must've been a terrible guide. Everyday he was getting down on my mom and me, making me want to puke myself to death and mess up a few squeaky-clean, dick lickers along the way.

The "future" has never meant much to me anyway. I never understood when this "time" was supposed to kick in. Everything always stayed the same for me – a frigging drag or an all-day, all-night nightmare. How was I supposed to get to a future when some days I couldn't even breathe? It sure as hell doesn't mean anything now.

My whole life, or what I can remember of it from when I was little, has been just getting through a day without losing it – getting mad, breaking down, or just giving up. My dad, Tarkin, my teachers, the doctor, the cops, even you by telling me to record all this, feel good about doing your jobs. I can usually tell by the way people move and talk how they feel about themselves – and me.

I know most of the cops want to kill me, but it wouldn't be doing their jobs, unless I attacked one or something. Then they could do what they wanted and say they were just doing their job. I can tell that each of them would love to be the one to kill me. At least that way no one would be worried about trying to understand me or what I did.

That's bullshit too. *Understand?!* My dad paid so many people to "understand" me and they all told him they did, but they didn't. They even told *me* they understood me, as if that was supposed to "cure" me or something and I just looked at them, or away, so I looked satisfied with their kidding themselves. It made all four of them feel better if they thought they "understood" me as soon as possible after meeting me. Then they wouldn't have to ask me real questions having to do with why I don't care about anything and why I do weird things. I never had to tell any of them that my feelings mostly went away a long time ago.

No one noticed or wanted to see me for who I am. I really knew that then. I'm not just making it up now to sound smart.

I could tell that adults especially, but some kids too, only wanted to go so far with me and no further. Most people and all adults have always seemed sort of afraid of me. At one point, it made me afraid of myself. If *they* were scared, I thought I better be. Then I just tried to drop it because they're all such gutless phonies anyway. I try not to put much stock in what adults do or say.

Once, I even told a psychologist in my first and last session that I wished I were dead and he leaned forward as if he were about to Hoover down a big meal and asked me why. I said I didn't know, so he told me I didn't really want to die and went on to talk about my burning ant hills. What an idiot! How does *he* know whether I do or don't want to die?

The wishing changed, though, to where I just wouldn't mind *being* dead. Dying scares me, but *being dead* doesn't seem too bad. Just suddenly not here, without everyone telling you what to do and never being good enough for anything except to be ragged on for having a short dick or getting bad marks or whatever. I wouldn't mind just being gone and having someone pretend they knew me or had figured me out and then speak about me around the world.

Maybe that's why you want me to say my thoughts and feelings on tape, if I had any. Maybe you want to say later that you understood me and give speeches about how screwed up I was. Maybe you just want me to get started in therapy, and you're too busy right now, so I'm starting alone. That's fine with me. Or maybe you just want to keep me busy so that I don't freak out and get laid by a cop again.

That's a joke. You wouldn't even think of that. You've never had it in the ass by a cop. Probably not by anyone else either. I bet that kind of stuff never comes into your head.

Just like my teachers and my father, that stuff doesn't exist, so no matter what I would say, if I would, and I wouldn't, you'd think it was for shock value and ask me whether I liked sports. I know about these things.

Just because I'm a great liar doesn't mean I don't tell the truth. In fact, sometimes I lie because no one believes the truth.

And even if they do, they pretend they don't. It's sort of hard to explain. But I've kind of lived by it most of my life, for what it's worth.

It's gross here, but it's okay — better than school and a little better than home. Basically, they leave me alone. They have to until someone important tells them what to do with me.

"What am I going to do with you, Harold?!" my mother used to say. I wish I could have told her. I would've if I could've. I wish I'd just made her proud of me once or that I was a genius or a super athlete so my parents wouldn't be so embarrassed by me.

My sister Jessica understands me, I think, and treats me pretty well. She's away at college, though, so I don't get to be around her much. I like her even though she does everything right and has never gotten into trouble. My dad calls her his "princess" and I'd hate her if I thought she liked it. But she doesn't really. She just humors him. She knows how to get what she wants from him and I love to watch her at work.

She even got a new car to have at college. My father thinks she's so "responsible." I wonder if she's been screwed yet. She's 19, so I bet she has. Seems weird, your sister screwing. Almost as bad as thinking of your mom screwing. I just hope Jessica doesn't go out with any cops. I don't want my sister getting it in the ass and, if you ask me, that's where cops like it.

This place really does stink. And if I say it stinks, it mustn't be fit for human life. Some of it is me, I know, because I haven't brushed my teeth since before school that day and my breath smells like barf and blood.

I haven't showered either, not since they brought me in and hosed me down like a sweaty horse. I can smell my B.O. Usually you can't smell your own B.O., but others can, and, at my age, they tell you. My mom tells me, or told me a lot before she just gave up because I never did anything about it.

Truth is, I like my B.O. and I go as long as possible between baths. It's sort of a statement to me. It *is* me. People
even complained to my mother about it. Some neighbors and
all my teachers since fifth grade complained about my stink-
ing. So did the cool guys at school and some of the girls. They
don't even just call me names and block their noses like ordi-
nary assholes – they actually complained to the office.

Can you imagine? "I'm sorry to bother you, Sir, but there
is something festering in this school. Something so toxic that
we might all die from the fumes! Harold Connally's B.O!"

Tarkin even took them seriously, tried to look important
like a general taking drastic action or something. He called
me down to the office, but he couldn't stand the smell, so he
sent me away and just phoned my mom. I think it's weird that
we're supposed to never stink, or we're supposed to put cheap
perfume stuff over our stink so that we don't stink. Then we
bring everyone's fake stink home with us everyday and we can
never cover it up, even with paint remover. It just cakes on us,
in layers, until you want to scratch yourself to death to get
down to your own.

In fact, you do everything for a world that stinks, including remove your own stink, so that you can come back to where
you are supposed to live with a new, strange stink, not even
your own anymore, but someone else's, everyone else's. No
one gives a damn here if I keep my own stink. I like that. I
don't even really mind the old stinks left behind here. It's not
the same as living stench. It doesn't fester. It's like just sitting
dead, not alive, and not getting worse. I can live with that,
but I probably won't. Someone with power is always planning
something for kids, especially for a kid like me, even before all
this happened.

Planning, which adults talk a lot about, never helped me.
It didn't help me to have friends, or make anything better,
really. I had no friends because of me. I mean I can be on good
behavior and all, and sometimes my dad even gave me money

to take kids some place, like the arcade on a Saturday and stuff. He thought I didn't know that it was a kind of bribe to get kids to want to be with me. Usually, I just spent it myself, on movies, bus rides to the mall and back, whatever. There was no point in wasting it on other kids.

Friendship never worked for me and, anyway, I don't believe in it. Also, there just never seemed to be a good reason for it. My whole life I've been a screw up, with everyone either pissing on me or ignoring me. So what's the point? When I would try to please someone, or get them to like me, something always went wrong. I'm jinxed, sort of. I don't know what you'd call it.

I don't want to sound cursed because I don't want to sound like I get a period every month like my sister and mother. That would be too gross. My mom told me that girls get weird for about a week before they get it. I can sure relate to feeling weird. Sometimes I just want to explode and blow everything and everyone away just to have some peace and quiet.

I don't want to cry, though, or I don't think I do anyway. I either feel anger or nothing at all. I actually thought a tampon in the trash was a dead mouse once, but even that didn't make me sad — just scared. I hoped that no one I lived with was into killing anything so violently.

Even as a walking screw-up, I knew how to kill things better than most, if you must know. It didn't have to be messy, but it could be if you wanted it to be. Like when I went a bit crazy and pretended to kill a rabbit and left its head on the kitchen counter. Mom almost had a heart attack, but she never told Dad. He would've had *my* head.

I've done other stuff too, but I can't tell you like this right now because it's kind of strange behavior for a kid, even a screwed up kid who's not supposed to be screwed up because he's from a normal family.

By "normal," of course, I mean my dad lived with us, he made good money as a school board consultant, my sister goes to university, and my mom is a substitute teacher. So, they were both kind of teachers with education and all. Since it's only outside that counts, we are definitely a good family. People always wondered about me because of that. They always wondered why I was so weird, or different, and smelled when I was from such a good family. Jessica didn't smell and wasn't a screw up. What was wrong with me? Wrong — that's what I am. W-R-O-N-G and always have been. Ask my dead dad.

I've also done some amazing things! I'm even kind of famous now, but not the right way — not the way that would please my dad. Who knows? I handled myself pretty well. And I used everything he taught me. He always said a man wasn't a man unless he could shoot a good rifle and kill what he aimed at. He said it was good if you could eat what you kill, but not necessary. He talked about Vietnam and all that stuff, even though he didn't go because of his weak eyes or something, but I heard him talk about some battles a few times as if he'd been there. He even said something to a guest once about some guy dying in his arms. What a bunch of crap!

He did the same thing when he watched football. He'd scream and curse and yell, "Kill 'im! Kill 'im!" as if it was gladiator hour or something. He'd give instructions no one heard or cared about. I'm sure a few guys he knew, and their wives, thought he'd been a football star too, along with everything else he pretended to be.

I remember being little and stupid enough to believe him, or at least to want to see him as big, powerful and experienced at taking guys out who might want to hurt us. But then I learned, partly by watching my mom, that he was a wannabe everything, even a wannabe killer.

He'd say, "Don't test me, boy. Just don't test me!" when I'd do something wrong, but I wasn't thinking of giving him a test or anything. And he'd yell, "Don't push me, Catherine! Don't push me!" at my mom, and she'd shut up even more than she already had. She'd almost stop breathing as if he might smash her head into the fridge or something. I'm sure he was a fake rough guy, but it's hard to tell. I'm sure even my mom never knew for certain what he'd do if he was really, really mad.

Once at the firing range, when he made my mom come watch, which she hated, he suddenly turned his rifle on me and yelled my name. My eyes must've popped out of my head and I squirted pee into my pants. I thought for sure he'd do it right there in front of my mom.

She screamed like *she'd* been shot, and the officials came from the office and my dad got all chummy and told them he was just kidding. There were rules against that sort of thing and that was a big one. They wanted to suspend him from the range for a month, and he got all embarrassed, but tried to look cool and smarter than them to talk his way out of it.

My mom and I knew to move off and pretend to be looking at the trophy display because we knew he'd want to kill us if he knew we heard him catching hell for being such an asshole.

That day, we all kept our mouths shut going home. He made us get in the car real quick and slammed the doors about a hundred times. All the way home, he swore at anyone, anywhere near our car, and passed everyone and went through yellow and red lights like he was proving he was a race car driver or something. It was kind of scary and kind of a high at the same time.

As long as he didn't aim a gun or the car at me, it was real interesting to watch my dad act like a killer. You'd sure think he was for real and stay out of his way – no question – but usually when he was going mental in the car, there'd be some other guy in the same mood and then things really heated up.

My mom and I would make sure our seatbelts were on and sort of crouch down in case we crashed or the other guy shot at us or something. The other guy was probably a fake killer too, so luckily we never actually crashed into anyone or got crashed into or blown away. He wouldn't want to show it, but my dad was always relieved just like us when nothing came of his acting crazy with other crazy drivers. It was as if he had to take this crap as far as he could, but didn't want to get killed.

Mostly he made his own rules, bullshitting and all, and when it came down to it, I think it was all in his head and he was really scared to death that someone might be as angry as he was and make him pull it off. I always wondered if he'd take it too far sometime, when my mom and I weren't with him, and he'd get mashed head-on in a bad crash. The asshole would've died alone for being out of control angry and pretending he was someone to be reckoned with and all.

Funny, it was always my dad who told me to never aim a gun at someone unless I meant it, and to keep my emotions in check. It was as if he was in a pretend war or something, one full of chicken-shit killers going around scaring each other and then later meeting for a stupid bridge game at one of their houses.

It's like adults playing video games where you get to mash each other, but nothing's real. I don't have any video games, but I'd bet anything they're less dangerous than playing war with real people, even if they are all fakes and all have secret plans on how not to get killed.

TWO

Home Alone

I KNOW I TALKED ABOUT my family already, but it wasn't the full story. Just like when everyone talks or complains about me, it's never the full story.

I must've done some good things at some point, but I don't remember anyone talking about them except for about three days after my last therapy session. I guess the therapist told my mom and dad that I needed positive reinforcement.

My parents tell everyone they're all for it, but I never had them try it out on me until that week a month or so ago. About three times a night, they'd come find me and ask what I was doing and tell me how great I was for doing it. I thought they'd lost it. It was so phony, like the way they are with their friends, suddenly all liberal and open-minded about stuff.

Once when I was jacking off, if you don't mind me saying, my dad opened the door to my room too quickly after his light knock approach and I whipped my hands out from under the sheet as if they were on fire or something.

I looked at him and he looked at me and he asked me what I was doing, even though it was obvious. I said I was just lying there trying to remember when my grades started to drop to try to turn things around. He nodded, pretended not to see the tent created by my excited and now pissed off dick and said, "Good stuff, son. Very good stuff. Keep it up."

Then he did the thumbs-up thing he does all the time with other people. Of course, after he closed the door, I couldn't. I wish he had been making a joke about keeping it up and all, but I bet he didn't even know what he said or how funny it could be if he could only be real for a minute, or knew how to be funny. Except when he flipped out, he was always acting. He acted like a progressive-type parent and adult. He kind of considered himself a leader of things and that's one reason I made him sick. I'm a loser.

By the time I went to my first therapy session, I didn't have any friends, let alone anyone to lead. Soon after, most people didn't even talk to me, except to call me loony, crazy or "Harold the Whack," as in whacko. I mostly just hung out by myself, which was okay with me, but not with my dad.

Sometimes, and I know I'm right, I could feel his whole body tense up when I walked into a room. He had to fight to keep from blowing up and screaming about how ashamed he was of me. I can't say I ever blamed him, but it was all too tense for words. Sometimes I tried, for his sake, not to breathe around him, to become invisible so that he wouldn't feel so bad. I never knew what else to do, except kill myself which, of course, I thought of and even sort of tried a few times, but it didn't work or I never pushed hard enough to actually die. If my dad knew, he'd say I was a failure at dying too.

I feel sorry for my dad, even if he is a phony and a snob about where people come from and all. He never thought he'd have a son like me. He'd say, "I never thought in a million years that I would end up with a son like you!" I know it made him sad and a bit crazy inside that he didn't have a son who could grow up to be what *he* wanted to be and pretended to be, but wasn't.

I think he wanted to be kind of Clint Eastwood calmed down by electric shock treatment turned into Bill Clinton, the handsome, smart and powerful sex maniac. Yeah, I think that's who he sometimes thought or pretended he was – Clint Eastwood, I mean. Even though he was just an ex-teacher, and didn't have — what do you call it? — oh, an Adam's apple. He really doesn't have one that you'd notice. Neither do I, but I'm surprised my dad hasn't had an implant or something.

I bet my dad believed what they say about guys with big Adam's apples having big dicks. I think it's pretty certain. It's funny that Clinton's Adam's apple isn't so big, so I guess his prick isn't either, but, well, I guess it doesn't matter when you're a president. Anyone'd blow you. Anyone. *I* might, if he could make me a hero or something and make people think I was important, not just whacko Harold.

I bet even my dad would approve in a sick sort of way. "Guess what?" he'd say to his associates at the school board. "My son blew off the president the other day and now he's a member of the Security Council. We're very proud."

My dad sometimes told my mother that he thought I was a fag. Just because I didn't hang out with a girl or anything, he thought I was a homo. This is another way he isn't as cool as he pretends to be. He wasn't against the state making it okay to be homosexual or anything, but he sure doesn't like them, or want them to live close by or get married or anything weird like that.

I mean, I wouldn't want to be given head against my will or anything, but all the fags I know are scared anyway and wouldn't dare try to make it with you. Jackson Saskel, if you can believe his name, is a fag. He goes to our school and gets pushed around a bit, but ever since people said he was a homo out loud, everything calmed down. It was like, "Who cares?" Like, if he didn't want us to be one, and he didn't get a crush on us or something, so what?

Sometimes the cool kids tease him about finding some

guy cute or something, but they basically leave him alone. Left alone, he's a nice guy. You just don't hug him at basketball games or other stuff in case he gets a boner and wants more. Since I don't hug anyone, I'm pretty safe in that way anyway.

Still, unless my dad finds me going down on a cheerleader under the back porch he's going to think I'm queer, to use the word he uses. I couldn't do that even if some girl would let me. What a thing to have to do to prove you're not gay! It's like guilty until proven innocent – gay 'til proven straight. What a drag! I'm not ready to grab a girl just to prove that I like them. None of them like me anyway, so I'd get arrested for sure.

It's actually kind of funny. I go near them and they huddle together like hens and whisper at each other, staring at me as if I might rape them all in one mad octopus' poke. Maybe that's good. Come to think of it, I should re-check the size of my Adam's Apple when you come back. Maybe I do have one. There's no mirror here, so I can't look at myself.

Again, adults in control think they know everything. No mirror because I would take it and slash myself and bleed to death. They'd never think I might just want to sneak a look at myself.

I couldn't possibly tell you about all the trouble I have gotten into. Plus, I'm waiting to know you better before I go as far as I could to at least try to do this speaking project you gave me. All I know about you so far is that you married a Jewish guy and went from Webster to Rosenthal, and that you pronounce your first name, Sandra, as if it were spelled Saundra. You're pretty young, as far as doctors and shrinks go, and so far you don't sound anything like my parents or teachers. You might be sort of nice, not too fake like most people, but I'm not sure.

The first night, even though you asked me what, I must say, were kind of stupid questions and left in a damn hurry, which was fine with me, you didn't get all sucky with me and you didn't seem afraid, just kind of mad or stunned or something. This morning when you came to talk to me a bit, you gave up instead of staring at me like other shrinks do. And you didn't seem disgusted or pissed off like I was wasting your time. You just said goodbye and that you'd be back.

I mean, you couldn't very well call me a little murderer like everyone else does, especially the cops. I mean, I know you're not allowed to call screwed up kids names when you're sent in to help or, as you called it, *assess* them. Maybe you wouldn't have anyway. I mean, I'm not sure or anything because I've been wrong so many times before when someone was nice to me and then tricked me or set me up or something.

Maybe I'll tell you stuff sometime if I know for sure you don't hate me and aren't laughing at me. But maybe I won't, so don't count on it or anything.

I like that you brought me a sandwich and the guard gave you a dirty look because everyone else wants to kill me or watch me drop dead from shock over what I did. You acted as if I got hurt in some way, and talked to me plain like, as if we just met and you knew I had just been in a major train wreck or something and might be scared and sick in the gut about it.

I know I didn't say much, but I remember how you weren't treating me like a murderer. You weren't thinking I'm something gross or dangerous, not that people think that's anything new just because of what I did. People, who I don't think much of, if you want to know the truth, always treat me like a thing, like an unpredictable, creepy dweeb.

My parents, more my dad than my mom, my teachers and especially kids, think that I'm – what do they call it? – oh yeah, synthetic or something. Like I was manufactured or made from weird chemicals, not born like everyone else with feelings. I mean, like the last three or four years or so, I didn't, but that's because I would've died if I did. So, I didn't.

I think I didn't have real, "normal" feelings anyway, and that's how people treated me even when, as far as I know, I did once feel sort of like other people do. I must've decided to scrap them or something. I can't remember.

Can you follow this or have you fast-forwarded? I wouldn't blame you. I know enough to know that I'm real boring. I'd probably freak out if anyone, especially adults, ever listened to me for more than ten seconds. I never knew how to put things so they'd sound interesting enough, or whatever, to get someone to listen, or even just half-listen as they did something else to not waste their time just listening to me.

Kids listened sometimes, if what I said was weird enough. Otherwise, it wasn't worth it. I could get kids to listen if there was "entertainment value" in what I was bullshitting about. I finally just accepted that no one listened. I had most of my best conversations with myself.

Okay, back to the troublemaker in me. Just ask my teachers and the cops. I'm sure that's part of what you're doing and maybe that's why you said you would see me in a few days. You'd be getting an earful.

For as long as I can remember, all I heard my parents talk about is "what they were going to do with me." When I was really young, like three or something, I thought they were going to auction me off with some stupid antiques or have a garage sale and put me in an old trunk. I even had a nightmare that they poisoned me with a poison that couldn't be found in the body once you died and I was real careful eating after that.

I didn't eat my school lunches for a whole year in case there was rat poisoning or something in the Spam. I got food poisoning anyway. I got it from eating in the school cafeteria. Since no one else got sick, I started to think that someone was trying to poison me there too.

I didn't think my parents would put out a contract on me or anything, but there are lots of people at school, including screwed up teachers who hate teaching, that I could see enjoying my suffering. Some tried to get me by totally embarrassing me in front of other kids. They'd ask questions they knew I didn't know the answer to, or ask my opinion about things they knew I was ignorant about – like friendship or the benefits of sports. Everyone would snicker and I learned to just lower my head and smirk.

They wanted to make me cry so that they could talk to me later and say sorry, but I wouldn't do it, not since I learned how to handle them, especially the ones who got their tits and rocks off by making pathetic kids seem even more pathetic. Even sicker, they sucked up to the cool kids and acted as if they were their buddies and gave them extra time for projects and stuff. The cool kids knew what they were doing and took the perks, but they mocked the stupid teachers behind their pathetic backs.

I still say kids are smarter than adults. Seems like adults get some little degree, or just get a little bit of power, and all of a sudden they think they're smart or have a handle on everything. If you want to know the truth, this has always scared me because they make the decisions and handle emergencies and stuff.

I even knew how they'd be that day. And I was right. They weren't even around. Ten minutes before, they were all over the place. You think kids are allowed to hang out all alone in the cafeteria? There are always a few teachers there in case someone punches someone out or gooses someone or chokes on a french fry or something.

As soon as there were shots and as soon as everyone was sure there was a shooter, the teachers kind of disappeared. At least from what I could see, which wasn't much. It was the kids, not the assholes, but the kind of low profile kids who didn't run and who tried to help.

I always knew teachers were afraid of us, underneath it all. And I knew they were, in a way, what my dad would call predators when he pretends he knows so much about hunting. They preyed on us to feel okay about themselves, the cowardly jerks. And they're supposed to protect us.

In fact, if they'd'a protected me instead of screwing me around like the rest of the world, they wouldn't've had to run and hide to save their own skin.

"Prevention is everything," my health teacher always said about getting sick generally, or from all this sex we were supposed to be having. What a joke! Give them an inch and they'll provoke you right over the line and then pretend to be shocked and think up new ways to describe how they might have seen this coming. They bloody well know!

They've always known kids like me, but they go at us and at us in front of other kids until we crack one way or another. I think they even enjoy being able to be there to look comforting and strong and professional after kids get hurt or in trouble or something, especially if parents are around, or visiting teachers, sometimes even newspaper guys and stuff. It takes their minds off teachers' strikes, the fact that they are useless, fed up adults, and that they are just dumb, older kids teaching younger ones to be just as dumb. I see most of them as yellow-bellied, control freaks. If they weren't, they'd control something more or bigger than scared kids with zits.

To this day, I'm not sure what my mother thought about my being trouble, except that I always hurt her and could never make her happy, which I would've liked to do.

When I was little, she called me "trouble on wheels." She'd say it to me, joking kind of, and sometimes when she didn't know I could hear, she called me that to her friends. She sounded stressed and all, but kind of like she liked me at the same time, as if I was normal then, just "difficult." I think it came later that she decided I couldn't be fixed. I'm not sure because she would never say that to me, like my dad did all the time, but she might've thought it.

She actually said less and less to me over the last two years, except when she went all psycho with excitement when a shrink told her I was doing better and would be just fine. Usually, especially lately, even with them both telling everyone I was getting better, she tried not to look at me.

It's weird, but I know she was trying to care for me, but not look me in the eyes at the same time. I helped her by not getting caught face on. When it happened, and she would look at me, she looked so sad, I felt crazy with anger and guilt and, I don't know, totally helpless because I didn't know how to just "straighten up" like my dad ordered me to about 4,000 times a week. If I could have, I would have – for her.

I felt terrible and I knew she wished she hadn't had me and that made me feel really bad feelings. I would've cracked my own spine to be straight for her. She didn't deserve to have a messed up, bent out of shape, goon squad for a son. Neither did my dad, but in a way, he kind of asked for it by lying to everyone that everything was so perfect in our family. He always told her, my mom, that it was her fault that they were stuck with me and that they "sure made a mistake on this one," meaning *me*.

She never said it, and even told him to keep his voice down a few times so that I wouldn't hear. I did, and wondered why they didn't just put me somewhere for adoption. I'm unfit to be a kid, whatever that means, whatever a kid's supposed to be. I just am. I'm not sucking around or anything about this. Really — I don't know any other way to be.

I wish she had defended me or said that she was glad she had me, even if she wasn't. But she never did and that made my chest ache.

Adults say the stupidest things and then they say *kids* say stupid things. At least kids usually know that they're being ignorant and are doing it for a reason. Adults don't even *know* what idiots they are when they open their mouths. Or they just don't care what they say to their kids because they think they own them or something.

I don't care anymore that my dad hates me. I mean how long can you care and get nowhere? So, like other feelings, I got rid of them. Now I just have a stomachache all the time, and my head's always pounding as if it's swelling up and going to explode. My mom says it's the flu. Sure, a three-year case of the father flu!

She knows, if you know what I mean, but just says these stupid things anyway to make things seem better. I get migraines too, but she says those are from changes in air pressure or something. I know she knows that my dad is an asshole. She pretends that he's this great community leader and stuff, just like he does, so that he doesn't criticize her as often as he would if she showed that she sees through him.

He made quite a bit of money from investments using a little bit of money he got from a great aunt or something, but he's always reminding me that shrinks cost a fortune. Ha! What a waste! I told him it wasn't doing any good, but he would get all buddy-buddy with them and show them how educated he was by speaking all that psychological stuff as if he were a shrink himself.

He also talked about my therapy at dinner parties and used terms that no one else understood so that someone who was really drunk would think he went to school to be a shrink or something. Women loved it. They'd tell my mother how lucky she was to have such a deep and sensitive man for a husband. My mother would fake-smile, mumble something, and find something she had to do in the kitchen as he went on and on with his stupid noise.

Once, after they'd had a fight, she made a break for the can and puked up the meal she made. She knew my father was a joke. She was just cool enough not to admit it to me or my sister.

Jessica bought the crap anyway. He had already convinced her to go to medical school and said that when she graduated he would give her a house. What if she didn't? Would he run her over with his "ride 'im cowboy" lawnmower? Probably, but she didn't get that about him, or she shut it out or something.

I prefer not to make bargains with adults, or with anyone

for that matter. You get bribed by the good part, but no one ever tells you what happens when you don't come through. She will, though — come through, that is. Jessica's real smart and has bought all this stuff about total security and what he loves to call "social standing." He likes to point out that only a small portion of the world's population has *real* social standing. What do the rest of us have? Squatters rights? Ditch deeds?

I was less than him and so was my mother, the truth be known, but he knew he could make a princess out of my sister, which is sad because she's really nice and asks me questions and stuff and shouldn't be blackmailed and bribed, even if she does go along with it. She keeps secrets I tell her and I respect that, if I respect anything. She never once told on me, even when I got caught trying to steal a boom box from Stereo Heaven. She just came down and paid for the thing and told them some story about my having seizures and blackouts and times when I didn't know what I was doing.

The guy wasn't too pleased, and I don't think he believed her, but he didn't call the cops because my sister was so nice and seemed to care so much. So, basically, she got me off. She told me that I had to pay her back, though, and I'm still trying to. Even though I don't know how I'm going to do it. Even if I have to rob some guard when he's not looking, my sister and I will be even, that's for sure. If she gets a lot of money now because something happened to them, I'll still pay her.

It's the principle of the thing, and I've always had principles unlike almost everyone I know. They don't count for much when you're weird though, or when you do things that scare people. People are so stupid and see everything in black and white. People think you can't have honor or ever tell the truth or care about anything if you do weird things.

This is such crap. It's the kind of stuff that has always made me want to smash faces in or, in my mind, spray line-ups of stupid, smiling and condemning adults with mushroom caps. I have some for my dad's Barretta. In case you don't know, they're bullets that pierce the flesh like needle missiles and then puff out inside the body like parachutes. They can tear the insides out of an elephant, let alone some stupid asshole's pee brain!

I don't feel too good. I'm going to stop for a while. I feel . . . I'm kind of shaking and my head hurts. I want to scream, but they might hear me. I have to lie down.

⋘⋙⋘⋙

I just needed to sleep. I think I can do a bit more now as long as I stay away from certain subjects, like being helpless and stuff. I hate being helpless and dependent on assholes who hate me. Anyway, forget that for now.

It's hard for me to forget some things. I've always had nightmares about certain kinds of stuff I'd like to blank out of my memory. I'm trying now. It's just that it's all swelling up inside me like a slow burn or something, climbing up at me from my gut. I've felt this way before. But this is worse.

I get scared and can't breathe and start to feel crazy. It even happened in school once so bad that a teacher gave me a brown paper bag and told me to breathe into it, slowly, until I didn't feel so crazy. Everyone laughed at me breathing into this bag, but it kind of worked. I keep some in my bedroom now. I wonder if they'd let me have some here.

Remember the rabbit? And the rabbit head? After they found the rabbit I said I'd blown up in the backyard, they told me that if I didn't straighten out, they'd send me away. It was already dead. I mean, I didn't chase a rabbit, catch it, shove a firecracker up its ass and kill it. I just wanted to blow it apart to see its insides. It was messier than I thought and when I was down at the lake washing guts and stuff off my face and arms and my Detroit Red Wings T-shirt, my father snuck up from behind and grabbed me and threw me against some damn sharp rocks.

He asked me what the hell I was doing, which he already pretty well knew. He lectured me for about six days. I went back later to get the head. I hid it. It was perfect, like it hadn't died or been messed with by a firecracker. I respected it – the head, that is — for surviving. And to look at it, you wouldn't think for a second it minded being dead. I guess because it never saw its body all messed up. Died of natural causes, which could be almost anything except a blast from a firecracker.

My dad could lecture on anything, including lawn mowing or pencil sharpening, until you thought you were going to go brain dead. He loved lecturing. Mostly, he loved the sound of his own voice, and he could say the same thing a thousand different ways.

Funny, he loved it and the rest of us couldn't stand it, especially when he was lecturing on the obvious. Looking back, I think he was a power freak. He should've been Hitler or someone. Lecturing was a tool and a weapon for him. He always debated people for no reason, just to show them that he was way smarter and that he had 600 degrees or something.

He'd always say, "When I was at Duke. . . ." or, "Just before leaving Columbia. . . ." which made people think he actually took courses there. Maybe he did, but they were probably seminars or something, open to anyone, even to me if I wanted to take one.

About three years ago, a principal at the school he taught at checked up on just what education he *did* have. He had bullshitted, of course, but the principal was his friend, so they just made him a school board consultant at the end of the year. Everyone thought it was a move up, and he acted as if it was too. He started to act even more important like, and said he'd been wasted as a teacher anyway. Now, he got to write up what he said were great ideas for the educational system, and talk at meetings and all. He really got off on it.

I think he actually believes most of the crap he claims. It's one reason I think he hated us, especially me and my mother. We know most of what he says is made up, faked or exaggerated and he hates having witnesses.

He likes people to think he's perfect and my mother and me always knew he was a pathetic snot with no guts. I'm almost certain she did. She never said so, but I could tell. And so could he sometimes.

I often wondered if he'd kill us, drown us on a holiday or something, just to be able to go on with his games without any embarrassment from us. This is another reason I kept an eye on him. I didn't trust him. I could easily see him putting an explosive by my butt while I was sleeping or something and laughing at the mess I made when he blew me up. He would probably say it was just like me to be so full of crap and all.

He wouldn't be upset the way he was when I blew away the dead rabbit, mostly because no one would know what really happened. He would get a lot of support, which he would say he didn't need, from people he'd told I was already a mess anyway.

Plus, he'd have a good out. I do have this thing about homemade explosives and guns. In fact, he taught me how to shoot a gun and even gave me one for my ninth birthday. I got really good at target practice and he started to put me down about it. But I knew I was good, and I kept practicing anyway, even though he told me that wimps don't shoot guns. My mom heard him say this once and later I saw her checking her bedside table to make sure hers was still there, loaded. She kept it for emergencies.

I know I'm making my dad sound like a real asshole. He is, but it's not as if he didn't try some stuff to make us happy or "with it" as a family. If you look at the albums and stuff my mom collected, you'd see all kinds of okay pictures, like the one they showed on TV the night they arrested me. I could hardly remember it when I saw it. Some cop guys were processing me and watching the whole thing on TV at the same time.

There we were, my dad and I, fishing with my Uncle Collin, There's even a shot of the three of us sharing the credit for a 12-pound trout. We look like boy and man scouts out for a good old time together and, in a way, we were. Sometimes, when other people are around, my dad can act real nice and all, always saying the right thing, never yelling, and not even letting on that he thinks I'm lazy, weak and stupid. There are quite a few of those pictures, and in some of them I think I'm smiling for real. Sometimes even I got all caught up in my dad's pretending, or I wanted to anyway.

My mom was okay, even though I make her sound like a pathetic robot. It's just that she couldn't be bigger than him in any way. And she had no life. She had no world, just like me. She went to do stuff, came home, and tried to keep my father from crapping on her. She had this weird habit of sighing a lot, for what seemed like no reason. My father couldn't stand it when she sighed, especially when he was sitting beside her in the car, or taking his dishes to the sink, which he hated doing anyway.

He talked all that women's lib stuff, but he acted like my mother was his slave. Even if he couldn't find his socks, he yelled at her as if she swallowed them or something. So, when he'd be right there and she'd sigh as if something was wrong, you could see he wanted to whack her.

Yet, all she did was serve him, take his crap, and watch him be phony with people they'd go out with or have in about once every few months. Nothing he ever did kept her from sighing, even though she tried to put a lid on it when she could see he might lose it. He'd either yell at her or go to his favorite chair in the living room and swear at her under his breath for an hour or so.

I always wondered why they called it that — a living room — because you weren't allowed to live there. Even with company, they asked them to take their shoes off, whether they were all dressed up or not. I sure wasn't allowed in the living room. No way. In fact, I don't remember ever sitting in that room, or even entering it. I would just ask something or answer from the doorway and keep out, as if it were private property, meant to remain empty, but open to others sometimes, like a funeral parlor.

My father went in there after dinner. There is this gross old armchair that he loved so much that he groaned every time he fell into it. It has a grease mark where his head lay back as if it were detached from his body. And he farted a lot in that chair as if that's what it was made for, even though it was always wiped clean and sprayed, untouched-looking for guests.

That's one reason I was glad I wasn't welcome in that room. In the evenings when he was home, it stank. Once, I saw and heard him do a few, and he actually raised one side of his butt and pushed them out. Then he sighed like he was a slave who'd picked cotton all day. I bet you could hear and smell it across town. I'm surprised there wasn't an investigation into the weird, evening pollution that hung over our neighborhood. It might as well of been a whale fart, and people should've been warned and told to spray that awful perfume stuff my mom sprays in the bathroom after he was done, which is another story.

My mother hated it, and when he deliberately forced a belch too. He could rock the house with a burp. Sometimes they were so loud and long that I thought he was going to puke up his dinner. He never did, but once he messed his pants when he over-pushed a fart. When he wasn't there, my mom said that she was damned if she was going to wash out a grown man's underpants every second day. She looked at me as if to tell me to keep my mouth shut about it. I did, of course, because what's the point of hurting my mom or telling my dad I know he shits his pants? For sure I never sat where he sat, especially in that chair in the farting room.

So you get an idea of an average evening at our house –
sighing and farting, sighing and farting, as if no one knew how
to speak. Sometimes my father would grunt, like if he wanted
more popcorn, or if the phone rang or something. Almost every night, even though they didn't like each other's weird habits, they usually watched TV in the room my dad likes to call
"the study," like it's full of ancient books or something. My
mom just calls it the TV room.

In addition to the sighing and farting, my father kind of
plays with and abuses the remote control for the TV, kind of
like whamming off a machine gun every three seconds. It drives
my mother crazy and makes her sigh even more because she
never gets to watch anything for more than two seconds at a
time.

Then, he gets bored and irritated and clicks the set off,
throws the remote on a footstool and goes to bed without a
word. My mom waits and then watches something, usually a
movie or one of those hospital programs, and relaxes. She only
starts sighing again when she has to go to bed.

And if you're wondering, I don't care if they ever did it or
not. I guess I sort of would care if I thought about it, so I don't.
Does that make sense? I mean, my mom seems so kind of frail
for his big, hairy body and I wouldn't like to think of him on
top of her, grunting and stuff. It makes me feel weird if I go
near to thinking about it, like I'd have to move out or something and never look at them again, which I guess I won't
have to.

If I had wanted a reason to kill them a long time ago, I
would've just concentrated on them screwing and my mother
trying to survive it. I'd rather my dad get it from prostitutes
than my mom. It just doesn't seem fair when he acts like he
hates her, but he has the right to just screw her whenever he
wants to and she has to let him because he pays most of the
bills. Then, he tries to act so cool around other women, like

he could have anyone he wants, and I know that sort of scares my mom sometimes when she forgets it's bullshit. I know I'd puke if he ever touched me.

I think my mom and dad hated each other in a way. I think they were really bored, and that's another reason they kept trying new techniques with me. I was like a project in a way. They were either in a truce, planning the next way to try to make me normal, or fighting over whose fault I was. I was like filler, or something, because they had such nothing lives, at least from what I saw.

Even though I was pretty much a disappointment and all, I don't know what my mom would've done without me. In a way, and I don't mean to be smart or anything, they were both kind of empty things walking, sort of pretending to live. Weird thing is, with the way they felt about me and what has happened and all, you wouldn't believe the number of times I wished I could make them laugh. I could never get them to look at me that way, or long enough without them getting all upset about something. We were always focused on bad stuff, or stupid stuff, or me being a total mess. I wish I could remember my mom smiling. But I swear to God I can't.

You wouldn't like what I'm doing right now. I'm peeing on the wall. I thought of using the piss and shit-stained toilet, but what's the dif? I'm going in a circle and pissing on all the stupid stuff assholes before me have written on the walls. I wasn't even born most of the years guys wrote this stuff. I know I'm going to catch hell for doing this, or they'll help you to decide I'm crazy.

One guy wrote so long ago I can't even read the year. Must've been a religious guy or a philosopher or something. He wrote in real nice handwriting: *There's no predicting the timing, just the inevitability of the eruption of a battered human heart.*

He'd be dead now for sure.

THREE

Shades of Gray

W HY DON'T THEY GET IT? Any of them – including you. Everyone keeps trying to find out what I think and all, and they keep trying to make it so, well, complicated and stuff. I don't know if I'm complicated, but I always knew I was different, sort of bad and sort of good, but I had something that could pass for a reason for everything I did.

I think that some people, especially kids, just handle things better — not that anyone really cares what *I* think. For example, I've always been a failure — in my own mind, not just my dad's or teachers'.

But some people I've watched can handle doing something wrong better than others, or at least better than I can. When teachers would get me on a point and give me a dirty look right in front of everyone, I'd almost puke with embarrassment. Everyone always made it worse by being either totally silent or kind of snickering with their totally cool friends.

Another guy could've had the same experience and laughed, even made the teacher laugh, and the whole class, as if they were ass-kissing little wit champions, but I always hid the fact that I felt like dying and blowing everyone away at the same time.

When I get humiliated and stuff, I can't get to sleep at night. To be honest, I'd stay awake and dream up all these tortures and things for the teachers and the assholes who laughed. I'd imagine tying them up and poking them with hot irons until they begged for mercy. Then I'd kill them with a semi-automatic handgun, Italian-made, the best.

I'd shoot and shoot, pumping bullets into them until they were just mush, and then I'd re-create them in my mind and start all over again with a new way to catch and scare them – and then kill them again. This was my bedtime and bus ride thinking for years, but I never did anything. It just helped to imagine it. In my mind, I could be real, and get respect and stuff, even fear.

It was the coolest feeling to exist and be noticed and reckoned with in a kind of bargain with people where, if they don't screw with me, they don't die. It was real clear like, and even made me popular because of the power. I miss those imaginings a lot.

I never told anyone this, but once I kidnapped a kid from grade school. I just kept the little shit for an hour or so, but it was still kidnapping. He was about five years old when I did it and I was ten. He was on his way home from pre-school and I just grabbed him off the sidewalk and brought him into the woods. I tied him to a tree and sort of got off on his whining for his mother.

He didn't say a word. He just kept crying louder and louder and snot dripped down into his mouth and his whole pudgy little chin and neck were covered with it. It looked like see-through blood or some kind of thick, snotty spider's web. He kept balling and balling and I got kind of bored and let him go.

I remember that I wanted to make him scream, not just cry. I wanted him to know that I could kill him if I wanted to, and that I might. He acted as if it was a bad game I was forcing him to play. Either that or he knew what I could've done and just cried waiting for me to do it. I don't know for sure.

I'd been watching him — actually him and his family. His dad played football with him in their yard where they had a pool and a barbecue and all kinds of cool stuff that made me think he was a spoiled little kid. He had a great mom, too. She was beautiful and spoke to him in a kind of gushy way, even in public and she touched him a lot, on the shoulder and on his face. It was pretty obvious that she loved him a lot.

Once, in the line at the grocery, I saw him lean against her thigh and wrap his arm around it as if he thought he was totally safe if he was attached to her. He had a brother too, but I didn't really know him. I just saw him once or something. I would watch their house at night and wish I could be in there with them. Even when they didn't know anyone was looking, they would do things together and laugh and hug a lot.

Before I kidnapped the kid, I had dreams of breaking into their house and scaring the hell out of them and then killing them, and making the kid's mother watch. I dreamed that she begged me not to hurt her children and the more she begged, the more I hurt inside, and the more I'd hurt her kids before I blew their brains out.

Afterwards, I hated those dreams. I even cried once, but not for them. I don't know why. But I think I liked being in them and doing that stuff while I was asleep. I liked being able to destroy their whole perfect life and listen to them scream because they were scared and loved each other and were going to become losers like me — massacred after a family outing to Baskin Robbins.

I have lots of thoughts like this. I can't stand fat, happy kids with mommies who tease them and dads who think their kids are the greatest things ever born into kidhood. It makes me want to puke, especially given the way they always looked at *me*. I was never too close because people have always backed off from me, but they looked at me that way anyway.

All the way from the other side of the schoolyard, some mom would get in her car and take one last sneaky look at me as she steered out of the lot. Early on, I realized that my weirdness showed. I mean, I've always known that I'm weird and all, but I never understood how others, especially cold adults, picked up on it. You'd think they could read my thoughts or something.

Even times when I wasn't feeling weird, they'd remind me with their cold eyes and with the way they hid their kids behind them as if I was going to hurt them or something. For a long time I got this gross taste in my mouth and choking dryness in the back of my throat when they'd give me "the look." It was sort of like having acid in my throat, so it was almost impossible to swallow, even though I would need to swallow more than ever. It almost never happens now. Plus, I don't look anymore. I banned eye contact two years ago. I don't look at anything too long or it starts to burn or turn to crap.

I learned a lot about keeping my eyes sort of glazed over and stuck in place at a school, if you can call it that, that my dad sent me to three years ago. He decided to send me to a sort of military-like place for a few years to "make a man" out of me. I was going to be a man as soon as I finished, and then I'd be alright. Well, it didn't work out too well.

Hawthorne Academy was what my dad told everyone was a prep school for the best universities and for officer's training in the army — like *I* was going to fit in there! I knew even before I went that I was dead meat, but he forced me, even bribed me by handing me a wad of spending money so that I could buy things at the tuck shop like the other guys.

I knew he was showing off again, even to the weird old guy who was not a principal, but the "Chief Officer." He wore this old uniform with medals all over it that I bet he bought through catalogues or something. He made us call him Chief, which I thought sounded like the name of a German Shepard. I called him that, though, especially in front of my dad when we went for the interview.

My dad answered all the questions and told him that I was an amazing athlete and student and everything, but I was under-achieving in both, so I needed more structure. I needed more structure like I needed more acid to swallow!

I also really needed to live in a squished dormitory with rich superstars about as much as I needed to be in a car crash! I asked him over and over if I could give my old school another try, but he wouldn't listen. I even begged my mother to talk to him about it, which I usually wouldn't do because he would give her hell and tell her to shut up.

I would've run away before I got kicked out, but I knew he'd take it out on my mother, and then he'd send me to some place worse, like a boy's farm where they do that tough love crap to straighten out asshole kids. So, I did everything I could to get out of it, but I had to go anyway. I knew I couldn't stop it. Anything my father ever started just kept going and going and going, no matter what, just like that battery commercial.

My father drove me up so that he could show everyone that I might become like him and came from good stock and all. He wore this tweed jacket with suede patches on the elbows – like some kind of Mr. Chips or something. I don't even know where he got it. Anyway, he sucked up to Chief so well that the old guy kept looking over at me and smiling and nodding as if he had an Einstein-Magic Johnson combo coming into his school.

He must've wondered, though. I mean, I'm real skinny, as you saw, and I've been told I look kind of expressionless, even dumb. I wasn't about to put on airs for this old weirdo. There was something about him that made me think he was a pervert or something. I mean, he had all these trophies and plaques all over his desk and walls, but his hands looked like a girl's. He even winked at me once and I wasn't sure whether he was saying he knew my dad was a phony, or wanted to do me. Anyway, I think he thought I was a fag. If not that day, then soon after.

My dad's lies got me in a lot of trouble because they made me seem normal or better. After reminding me how much the place was going to cost him, he left me stranded with all these bigger guys with classy clothes. Of course, I wouldn't be caught dead in them, but they showed me up right from the start.

Taylor, this rich guy from Philadelphia I had to room with, was the worst part. He was in with the prefects and spoke with a weird accent as if he was Prince Charles or something. As soon as I was shown my room, he laid down the rules and told me that he was getting some benefits for rooming with me.

If I screwed up or bugged him, though, he was allowed to break the deal he'd made with Chief. It was then I knew I was right. Chief knew my dad was a phony, took the money, and hoped I wouldn't be too much trouble. And this ass kisser was helping him out for points. Some things never change.

Well, you don't have to hear the whole embarrassing story, but they got me pretty quickly. They kept initiating me.

When I looked upset or pissed off, even though I tried not to, I got towel whipped about a million times before and after sports, which they never let me play because I was so lousy. I had to sit there on the bench and watch.

Thank God, in a way, because I swear one of them would've bashed my head in just to get points with Chief. While I was at Hawthorne, the guys short-sheeted my bed and put a dead squirrel in it, put Preparation H in my toothpaste tube and did a whole bunch of other stuff everyday. I never knew what was going on and couldn't ever get oriented.

The teachers just ignored me, as if they knew I wasn't someone whose parents they should suck up to or that I wouldn't be there very long. A couple of them gave me dirty looks on and off, but they didn't call me any names. In fact, they didn't call me anything. I don't think anyone used my name the whole time I was there.

I was just the new kid who was there for a reason differ-ent from everyone else. A few of them thought I might be psycho or something and just stayed clear. But mostly, when I wasn't being freaked out by an initiation, everyone left me alone.

The way I got kicked out was kind of weird. This one older guy, who I didn't see much on purpose, caught me in the can in the middle of the night and leaned over the cubicle where I was having diarrhea and peed on me.

I think he planned it because I had diarrhea every night and couldn't sleep, so I think he knew I'd be in there and told others he was going to piss on me when he caught me there some night. Well, he sure did. And he must've been holding his piss for a hundred years because it kept coming and com-ing and when I bent over and moved forward on the seat, he kind of did a diagram on my back. It was drilling into my back, all hot and sort of sweet smelling and I was shitting over the edge of the toilet and I couldn't do anything.

He was cracking up, and when he saw the mess all over my underpants and on my feet, he just about lost it, he was laughing so hard. When he was finished, he wiggled the last drops from his dick and climbed down from where he had wedged himself between the ceiling and the partition.

I just sat there, listening to him by the sink, still laughing and asking if I enjoyed the little "freshening up," or did I want some more to help clean up my mess. I didn't feel much, ex-cept that stinging, dry feeling I get a lot when something aw-ful happens and feelings would be too much. I remember stand-ing up, but not much after that.

I was told what I did, but it doesn't sound like me, if you know what I mean. They said I came out of the cubicle with my pants down, and with shit on my feet and legs, even on my dick, and that I grabbed him and pushed him into the cubicle where I'd gotten pissed on. I don't know how I could've, but then they said I pushed his damn head into the toilet which, by the way, I hadn't flushed.

They said that I held him there 'til he had to suck in crap and piss and then pulled him up and shoved him back in again, over and over until he was crying and whining for help. Then his friends came, a few prefects, then the campus cops, then the House Master, who didn't like me, but had to make them stop pounding me out to try to kill me anyway.

I was taken to the gym supply room until morning. They locked me in there all smelly and said that I'd meet with the Chief in the morning. Well, I knew what was coming. I knew they'd phone my dad and that I'd get killed for screwing up. That's when I thought of running away to South America. You know, to one of those places where old Nazis hide and no one can find them. Problem was, I didn't have any clothes, and I literally looked like shit. And, as usual, I stank, but worse than ever.

I almost ran away when they told me they had phoned my parents to come and get me at the end of only two weeks. They told me on a Monday, so I had almost four days to go crazy listing all the things my dad would call me. I knew if he came he wouldn't even bring my mom because, well, in the first place, she knew the place wasn't for me and felt bad I had been sent there and all.

But I also thought he'd want the two hour drive back home to be what he liked to call "quality time," meaning I was going to catch hell all over again for everything I'd ever done, and for the fact that I was a piece of useless shit to begin with. I knew he was going to say that I didn't have the balls to handle it or that I give up on everything and won't try.

All the same old stuff would be repeated in that way he has, with saliva around the corners of his mouth as if he wants to stomp on me and tear me into a million pieces. I felt like I couldn't take it, especially after being at the school with all those rich, macho, cool types who go there and are perfect at everything. I hoped maybe he wouldn't come and instead just wish I'd disappear out of his life.

My dad didn't come for me after all. I met with the Chief who, right after it had happened, wasn't going to let me shower, but then did because he started to gag when he came to talk to me. Within two days, I was given my clothes and most of the stuff from my room and driven to the bus stop with bus money from a year's tuition.

That's when I realized that my special Chicago Bulls illumination watch was missing and I knew pretty boy Taylor kept it. He must've kept my Swiss army knife too because I never found it in my stuff. I was real upset because I don't have too many cool things, but I wondered why he stole them from me. He had so much stuff it was amazing, and he could buy anything he wanted without having to do odd jobs the way I did. Maybe he's a klepto or something. Anyway, I missed the first bus and forced myself to get on the second at about midnight. I didn't have enough money to go to South America.

I was glad my dad wasn't there when I got home. He was away on business or just took off for a while so that he wouldn't have to do a life sentence for killing his kid. Probably he'd only get manslaughter anyway. Or probation. Once he'd explain to a judge how much I'd disappointed him, and how he did everything he could for me, the judge would probably arrest me for parent abuse.

As soon as I got home, I snuck right out and went to my old school to register and gave the guidance counselor an amazing story about why I wanted to be back at this terrific school. It was all garbage, but I told her I missed the kids in my class (who, by the way, had spread a rumor that I was upstate in a mental ward) and that I felt a general education was better than a sort of exclusive one.

She probably knew I was bullshitting her, but legally I had to be in school anyway, so I re-registered in the middle of the term. I mean, I hated school, but I had nowhere else to go

during the day, and if I didn't go to school I'd never see anyone but my parents, unless my sister came home or something.
Plus, I was used to life there. I could handle it, sort of.

I might even pull the head in the toilet stunt again if
anyone really went after me, especially now that I knew I could
do such a cool thing. In a way, I thought my dad should've
been proud.

So, when I was back, things kind of went back to normal,
whatever that is. Tarkin wasn't too glad to see me, but it
would've been illegal not to take me back. Just like my parents
– they couldn't just dump me somewhere, which I'm sure my
father would've done a long time ago if he could've. My mom
probably would've cried and made up some good arguments
for not doing it, but I know she wouldn't actually stop him. I
still felt kind of lucky to be in a place that I knew something
about, and where I knew who hated me, which included just
about everyone.

I know you want me to start working up to that day, but I
really want to tell you stuff before, too. I mean, I'll maybe try
to get to it and all, but, as I said before, I'm not just Harold the
murderer. I'm not.

It's sort of like the head in the toilet stunt. I didn't know
I could do it, but I did. I'm glad that I did, too. Or, at least I
was, once I believed I actually did it. That guy must be scared
of me now, hoping I don't come back. He thinks I'm whacko,
capable of anything, and I kind of like that. I heard later that
the old Chief had phoned my father to ask him to phone this
guy's parents and some parents of some of his buddies as well.
He wanted my dad to tell them that the school didn't deliberately admit psychos, that their standards were high, and that I
was some kind of aberration.

The last part was probably easy for him, but the first part
must've killed him. I must say that I don't really enjoy embarrassing him, but there wasn't much I could've done. I even
thought it wasn't too stupid of an idea to make me write the

guys and their parents and apologize. You know, I'd sound normal and responsible and all, so everyone'd calm down. I did it and I think it went over real well. They could relax and just think I'm a complete asshole instead of a maniac. Assholes, everyone knows, are pretty common. Most people, even so-called adults, think maniacs are rare. Another bunch of crap. They just hold it in.

At least I knew back at my old school who the assholes and maniacs were. I had to watch out for all of them. I went back to spending a lot of time in the schoolyard – instead of the cafeteria or library – between classes. I have always just tried to stay out of people's way. At least since I realized there was something weird about me. That way, I didn't get picked on as much and have to pretend I didn't give a damn and, also, I didn't get blamed for as many things as I would've if I'd stayed indoors.

In fact, some of the stuff I would be blamed for would be true. My whole life I've been prone to dropping dishes, accidentally ripping pages in books, and once I even choked and puked a sandwich halfway across the cafeteria into someone's Jell-O. In gym class, if we were forced to play a sport, I'd either break the equipment or smash a window. Doing stupid, basic gymnastics or even just sit-ups, it'd be me who farted and got ragged for it. So it was better for me to just keep to myself, outside, where there was lots of space to move around and away from things and other kids and teachers.

Of course, I could fart too and that was a comfort. It's a funny thing about farting. I know I talked about my dad farting and you might think I have this fascination with farts or something, but the whole thing about farts and burps confuses me. I read somewhere that a fart is the one thing that every culture in the world finds funny. And yet, if you happen to let one fly, you're branded for life!

There was this guy before me at school, like a hundred years ago, who farted during a gym display for parents. He was doing a somersault in kind of a domino-like thing with fifty other guys and there wasn't a sound in the room except for the guys hitting the mats and then this guy echoed one, bums up, right off the gym ceiling. One or two of the parents watching laughed a bit, but basically the whole audience just squirmed a bit and pretended it didn't happen.

But the guys laughed so hard the whole setup fell apart and they all ended up lying on the mats cracking up at this fat guy and his fart. From then on, he was the "fat farter." That's all. Nothing he ever did made anyone forget it. Even teachers taking attendance at the beginning of a new year would say his name, try not to laugh, and then the whole class would crack up. I heard the story so many times, I began to feel kind of bored when I heard it. Then I started to wonder what ever happened to the guy.

I heard he skipped all the grad stuff and just vanished. Then one day, during assembly, the vice principal asked us to have what he called a solemn moment for this guy whose name I'd never actually heard. He became an accountant or something, but snuffed himself out in his garage by closing the door and turning his car on while he just sat there. Apparently, he was all puffed up and yellow by the time someone found him.

When I heard that it was the fat farter, I felt kind of strange inside, scared sort of, but mostly I thought it was really weird that he killed himself with fumes. One long, car fart and he died. That's one of the things that got me wondering about lots of stuff early on. I mean, some things make no sense at all, and other things make too much sense. Does that sound right? I don't know.

Oh, I wanted to say thanks for coming this morning and telling me that I could take my time getting to what my dad would've called the "meat of the matter." I think you're supposed to figure me out as quickly as possible, but I really do appreciate your letting me do it as it comes.

I mean, you remembered that I didn't want to talk at all,

let alone into this hand-held techno listener thing, and that meant a lot to me. That you remembered, I mean. I know you're probably taking heat from that guy Spencer who's defending me because you're not finished, but you're not taking it out on me, which is kind of unique.

I also liked our talk about whether this place scares me and whether I'll be prepared to go to the new facility before the arraignment. I know I wasn't totally honest with my words, but I think you got the truth anyway. I'm scared and I'm not. I mean, you seem to get that I'm at the end of something, and I don't care, but I don't want to be screwed anymore either.

I also know I'm safer in here and wherever they put me next because everyone out there wants to kill me. Even my dad would, and he'd have a pretty good excuse if he weren't dead himself, which I'm almost sure he is. Funny, no one's told me anything for sure. Did either or both my parents *not* die? If one made it, I hope it's not my mom. I'd kill myself before I ever looked her in the eye again.

How many kids were hurt? Or worse? Whatever. They yell things at me, but one guard told me that I shot the principal or something and I'm almost sure I didn't. So, I don't know what's true. Come to think of it, that's nothing new. I always just assumed that everyone lied, but that some people don't know the difference.

That's one thing I know for sure — what's a lie and what's the truth. Truth is harder, by a million times, but bullshit can get complicated and can come out like truth, as if truth is too hard to figure out or something. I guess that's why almost everyone acts all the time, as if it's actually reality. It's just plain easier to bullshit and accept it back. Can you imagine if we all started to really tell the truth and others had to hear it and then tell the truth too? Damn, what a mess that would be! Like a war!

You said I could use whatever language I wanted when I started this and I pretty much have, but I feel kind of bad now when I use the "F" word and all. It's almost because you said it was okay that makes me want to try to cut down on it a bit. Also, you seem like, well, kind of sophisticated, as my dad would say, but down to earth at the same time. I really don't mean to insult you, or make you think I don't know better words to say things with.

It's just when I feel strongly about something, which is pretty well everything, I use gross language. See, at school, no one spoke to anyone out of class without saying "fuck" or "shit." It just wasn't normal to talk politely. I mean, no one made me talk dirty or be "foul-mouthed," as my mom would call it, but I sure would've been considered even weirder if I hadn't sworn and cussed and acted nasty a lot of the time.

I mean, with a name like Harold, you have to swear a lot just so that guys don't think you're going to ask them out or something. Ya know what I mean? Anyway, sorry for the language, but you said it was okay and you haven't lied to me yet, I'm almost sure.

I finished the year with really low marks, but enough to just pass, which was pretty well my regular score at school. My dad hadn't told me, but he had arranged to have me sent to Big Brother Y camp for the summer when I got kicked out of Hawthorne.

I was sick at the thought of it, which is probably why I got really sick and couldn't get up to go. My dad told me to stop faking and got me to the bus at the Y building with just my sleeping bag and a pair of jeans. Well, I puked all the way up on the bus and then, like a jerk, fainted when I got off the bus. The nurse saw me and got real scared and she called an ambulance to take me right back to the city.

They called my mother and she was there when I arrived looking all worried and everything, as if I might be faking and she was going to catch hell for doing what my dad called "enabling" me. But they needed her to sign something really fast because my appendix had burst and my body was full of pus and stuff and I was almost dying. I had to stay in the hospital for over a week because the thing had exploded.

My dad didn't come because I knew he thought I brought it on to get to come back. I sure didn't because I'm not that brave, and I thought I was going to die on the ride up it hurt so bad. But after, I was glad because then I sort of had the summer off.

When my dad finally talked to me, and he certainly took his time, he told me I had to find a part-time job and learn something. He also signed me up for the next level of target practice, which I liked and that sort of made him happy, but he wanted me to do something else, too.

So, I had to look around. When I finally found something, I thought my dad would be pleased, but he thought it was a sissy job, like hairdressing or something. I didn't think of it that way 'til I thought about it, and I guess you could say it was mostly a girl's job, but I thought I might like it anyway.

A new couple with little kids had moved into the new development by the lake and they advertised at the school and community center for someone to watch their kids during the day. All someone had to do was play with them, make some sandwiches for lunch if their mom forgot to or something, and take them swimming and stuff. And it paid $500 a month. I could even live there if I wanted, or cycle over real early in the morning and leave around dinnertime.

I didn't tell anyone that I phoned them and introduced myself and told them I would like the opportunity to care for their kids. I figured they hadn't heard all the stuff about me yet, and they might hire me if I was polite and if I told them that I really liked little kids, which is true.

They had a Golden Retriever, my favorite, and I told them I considered that a bonus, which was also true. I just hoped they didn't think I was messing with them to get the job because I really wanted it, so it might have sounded like bullshit.

Anyway, I waited for two days before they called and asked

me to come back on Saturday to see the kids again and learn about the house and the boat and stuff. Then they told me we'd all give it a go. That's how they put it — "a go."

I thanked them and they seemed real nice, and as if they liked me, and their kids, a two-year-old girl and two boys, four and six, seemed to like me, too. Probably because they sensed I could relate to them, all awkward and everything. Plus, they kind of respected me too or something because, to them, I was much older.

It felt cool and I didn't let myself care what my dad thought. And I sure didn't let anyone from school know or they would've mocked me and then made secret calls to Brendan and Megan, that's the name of the couple, to tell them what a creep I was. I kept my mouth shut, but I was really glad to have it, and to be sort of in charge of something important, like someone's children.

Things went really well for at least three weeks. It seems longer because I really liked the kids and I got to sort of run the house. I even cleaned up one night after Brendan had pulled a surprise birthday party for Megan and there were hundreds of people all over the property, dancing and drinking and eating up a storm. Brendan invited me, but I was too shy to actually go, so I sort of just watched from the bushes and stuff.

Then, when it was over and they had gone to bed, I sneaked in and quietly cleaned up. I swear Megan almost squished me to death the next morning when she figured out I'd done it. She hugged me and I could smell her hair and perfume and feel all the air leaving my body and my legs were tickling.

For a second, I thought I was going to have a boner, but then I realized the feeling was something else. I was glad the hug didn't go on too long because I'd never had that feeling before and I was sort of nervous about it. Brendan was happy too, and gave me a wink and slapped my back like he was my pal and all and it felt awesome.

The whole day with the kids I felt 400 feet tall! I've never, ever felt like that. I guess I never will again, either. But once was like being a completely different person, without all my insides churning all the time with only empty space to churn crap into. Just as I'm saying this, I'm thinking that it might have been pride or something I was feeling. All I know is I was higher than on any drug I ever tried.

Then Kerstin almost drowned. Yeah, she did, and she's the two-year-old. I was building a raft with a kite attached to it with all three kids helping. They were getting this and that for us and really into the project too, so I didn't think she would wander onto the short dock. Well, just when we were hammering, I thought I heard this splash, more like something light falling off a tree into the water, but I sort of looked around anyway.

I didn't see Kerstin. I started calling her and running in circles and, eventually, I ran over to the dock where she fell in. I jumped in, even though it was only two feet deep, pulled her out and put her on her tummy. I pumped water out of her and then turned her over and did all that clearing of the mouth stuff before I gave her mouth-to-mouth.

I was shaking and almost crying when she gave off this little cough and whimpered a bit. I hugged her and told her it was okay, that she was okay and all. I kept telling her that as we went in to get dry clothes and had a snack and Connor and Brendan talked about how amazing it was that I saved her.

I wasn't thinking about that, of course. I was thinking that I screwed up. Big time! I sat them all down because I was really scared and I told them we should keep this to ourselves, which was a stupid thing to do, and we all swore on a code of honor we made up. Kerstin bounced back, as they say, pretty quickly, and we had a great afternoon. It was like it never happened.

I should've known. I did really. It wasn't the kids' fault. They thought it was such a great story and were so excited by my saving Kerstin, that they told their parents who, as you can imagine, weren't too happy that she fell in *at all*. I had just arrived the next morning and leaned my bike against the side shed where I always left it.

Before I could go in, though, Brendan came out looking pretty stern and kind of upset and handed me a check. He told me it was too dangerous to have me there if they couldn't be sure I'd watch all the kids real careful. I just nodded and listened because I knew he was right, but I wanted to die. It's like something I'd never had before had vanished on me and I was an asshole again and being told to go away. I definitely wasn't welcome anymore.

As I turned to go back to my bike, I saw Megan and the kids watching from the kitchen window. Megan looked really dark, kind of offended or scared, as if I had said something really rude to her or threatened her. The kids looked sad. She shushed them away from the window when she saw that I saw, and the window went black, like their faces had never been there.

Brendan watched while I got on my bike and he nodded when I sort of whispered that I was sorry. I looked back as he stepped from the stoop into the house and closed the door.

As soon as I was out of sight, I got off my bike and sat on the side of the road. I never felt so bad. I didn't even care that cars were speeding by about a hundred miles an hour and I was getting covered in dust and gravel. I sat there all day 'til it was getting dark. I only got up after their 4-x-4 went by and they saw me and sped up, like I was crazy and might come back or something. I knew I better not be there when they returned.

I got home and couldn't close my eyes or swallow or anything for hours. Even my nose was all crusty with road dirt. It was like I had a dirt shell or something because I had to kind of chip it off in the shower. Mud from my hair poured down into my eyes and all over the shower floor and walls.

Funny, I didn't feel any cleaner when I had washed it all off and could blink again. I felt like a dirty, skinny scrub with nothing to look forward to again. I could've died.

Instead, I started figuring out how to explain why I wasn't going there anymore. I decided to buy myself a week by going somewhere else during the day. Then, I'd try to explain, knowing I'd have the same old stuff thrown at me about failing and being useless. All and all the experience almost killed me because I screwed it up, but I'm glad Kerstin was alright and that she saw me as her hero. I think of them sometimes, and try not to remember the dark window. I try anyway.

They were about the last people I really, well, talked to or had anything to do with. I can't stand that they're probably *really* afraid of me now, and think they were lucky that I didn't shoot them all over a barbecue.

I wish I could go back to that time. Right this minute, I wish I could go back. I'd hold Kirsten and tell her it's alright again. Things, all things, are never what they seem, I've found out. But everyone tells everyone else what things are to keep it simple and they all swear by one version. Then everyone feels more comfortable, even if it means hating people, even killing them in wars and stuff. I'm not trying to be smart or anything, but I've known for as long as I can remember that I'd always be one of the "easy to hate" kind. I just knew it. At least I was prepared.

FOUR

Momentum

I THINK I KNEW SOMETHING was going to happen. I can't be certain because I'm not a mind reader, even where my own screwed up head is concerned.

Things were just getting worse at home, worse at school, and it seemed that everywhere I went, which wasn't too many places, I got crapped on. It even got around that I tried to drown someone's baby, got caught holding her under water and everything, and then got arrested.

That really made me upset, especially because I liked them all so much and actually saved her, even though it was my fault she fell in. It really got to me, so I smashed one of our back windows with my fist. I said I was hitting balls, so all I had to do was pay for it out of my allowance and what I earned doing chores. No one noticed or asked about my hand, all bloody, swollen, purple and gashed, after I washed it off and all. I knew they wouldn't, so I got away with it real easy.

About a week before the thing happened, I was watching all these hot seniors practicing in the gym for graduation and prom ceremonies. I was hiding in the equipment room,

54

which was one of my favorite places, partly because it stank in there and no one could tell I was there, and partly because you could look through a crack in the door and see pretty well the whole gym.

There was even a hole under a junky table, about three inches off the ground, which showed a whole corner of the girls' locker room. I saw a whole lot of tits and pussies and stuff through there in my time. Once I got a boner and had to get rid of it when I heard someone coming. I mean, I could say I was looking for an old shirt to shoot hoops in, even though I never played basketball, but it wouldn't fly if I stood there with a popper in my pants. They'd know it wasn't a reaction to old basketballs and sweaty uniforms, even if it was me.

A hundred times, I bet, when I needed an excuse for something I was doing that I shouldn't of been doing, or wasn't allowed to do, I'd say I lost one of the little screws from my glasses. I'd get down on the floor, stay on my knees and look around for a while. Sometimes, I'd look for an hour in some places before everyone was gone and I could get up and leave.

Usually, I was really looking at something either private, like up a girl's skirt, or something fascinating, like bugs screwing. I love watching bugs screwing. I also like to watch them hunt together, ants at least. Soldier ants carry each other home and stuff when one can't make it. They can also carry huge chunks of stuff in their mouths, stuff way bigger than they are, and then eat it. I kind of admire ants, except that they're one of the easiest things to squish for fun, which a lot of people do. Kids, and even some dumb adults like the crackle, snap, pop sound of killing a real big one. Sort of a cereal death. Get it? Sometimes I try to be funny.

Anyway, I was watching and saw all these really sexy girls practicing walking and giving cute little acceptance speeches in case they were voted Prom Queen. Their boyfriends, which they all had, of course, were standing around waiting for them in their school jackets with sports crests all over them.

The guys were being kind of crude about what they did with their girlfriends, but the girls couldn't hear. They were all giggles and whispers, working toward their five minutes of fame in a small town gymnasium. Kind of dumb, but kind of sweet too.

I wish I could make things bigger and better than they really are, but I never could. Things just are what they are – usually boring and full of crap. There was always shit on the horizon, so close I could taste it. Guess that explains my breath.

There was one girl I kind of liked and, if you have to know, I had a few amazing imaginings about her. I dreamed once that she really liked me and asked me to go on a picnic with her near a private pond. In the dream, she kissed me real soft and touched my face with her soft hands. Then she held my head against her breast. I cried in a good way and she said everything would be alright.

I woke up with a hard-on and a headache. I usually woke up with a headache anyway, though. Especially after a good dream, the headaches were much worse because it was sad to go from something nice to a whole bunch of hours without anything to look forward to except maybe having a nice dream again. That's if I didn't have a really freaky nightmare. If I did, I woke up with an even worse headache, what my mom calls a migraine, and about a week of the shakes.

Sometimes I even thought people were talking about me when they weren't. I mean kids did that to me all the time, and so did their parents. When they thought I couldn't hear, they'd whisper that I was getting weirder or something, or that I was a pervert. So, it was hard to tell when I was imagining it and when I wasn't. To me, most things that I imagine are real and most things that are supposedly real don't seem right or possible to me. It's hard to explain.

Like school, it's more unreal than real to me. Sometimes I think I must be dreaming that I have to get up and get dressed and go to this fenced-in place with lots of rooms and move around to different rooms when bells ring. Then, when a long bell rings, I get to leave to figure out what to do 'til I have to go home. The long bell in the morning always makes me sick to my stomach and dizzy.

I get scared everyday when the bell rings because I have to sit in this room, have my name read, and maybe be laughed at for the millionth time and then move from room to room when more bells go off. Good practice for prison.

What's even weirder is that *adults* live like this. Teachers are such wimps. I mean, they leave school and the bell thing, and then they study to come back. And *they* can't go anywhere without the bells either. They can't leave at lunch like other adults. They look sick in the morning when we start, and relieved as hell when the last, long bell announces that they can prepare to get the hell out.

Grown-ups choosing to live in little rooms and hallways with a bunch of kids controlled by bells must be deficient or something. Or maybe the little rooms, schedules, bells and a trapped audience of stupid kids everyday keep them from losing it and blowing their brains out. Nothing like a little structure, my dad always said. "Keep it tight and maintain the fight," he'd say, and I'd wonder what we were fighting.

It's like everyday was a war for some people. For me, it was just a head game between them and me, and me and me. I just tried to keep my head from going to places that made me sick, scared, or so sad I'd puke. Like I sort of told you before, sometimes I'd even go to places where I gathered up all the assholes in my life and stabbed and poked them to death as they looked up at me and begged me not to hurt them. What a rush — *them* begging *me*! And none of them ever knew how they were cooking their own goose by begging.

As I told you, lots of times, before I went to sleep, I imagined doing this kind of stuff. The next day, when I'd see them for real, I'd look at who begged and got cut up or shot the night before and smirk at them. I have to say, when I smirked at them like that, they actually looked scared and didn't whisper anything about me. They just walked off in packs, which made it easier for me to imagine getting them all at once from behind with an Uzi or something.

You should know, though, that mostly I didn't think about violent stuff. I just did it when I was feeling humiliated or sorry for myself because none of the even semi-interesting kids would give me a chance to be a person. Just like my dad, they had their minds made up and acted one way in front of adults and another way when no one was looking other than their friends.

I often wanted to blow my parents away for the same reason – everyone pretending to know me, but never speaking to me or wanting to be with me. Sometimes I just couldn't stand it, and I felt this rush in my head and a queasy feeling in my stomach. This kind of stuff made me feel guilty and kind of ashamed, but I knew I'd never do any of it.

I honestly couldn't stop thinking about it because it's all I had, sort of, to feel like I had some force or something, like I at least existed. But only in thoughts and dreams. I would've never thought I would've actually done something like that to make myself real, or noticeable, or anything like that. I never would've planned a thing like that or thought it through. I'm not even brave enough. The truth is, I really don't want to be noticed. Never did, really. Not since I found out it always brought me trouble.

Tarkin suspended me. I hated him because he was always looking for some reason to get me. Once he even told me I closed my locker too loudly, as if I should put rubber lining around it or something. I'd end up having the only silent locker in the whole school and then he'd probably find something wrong with the way I did my combination or left fingerprint smudges on the dented metal or something stupid like that.

The day he had me suspended, my history teacher, Ms. Stockdon, who has one glass eye that looks the wrong way when she's trying to glare at you, told him I was chewing gum and wouldn't spit it out. She hated me too because I didn't study enough and made it pretty clear that I thought she was a lame freak.

I mean she wasn't actually lame or anything, but she spoke with a fake British accent and talked about her ancestors being royalty and all. The day Princess Diana was killed was a Sunday, and she stayed away the whole week, as if she was at the funeral or something. After that, all she could talk about was Diana, Diana, Diana. I mean, we knew what had happened and it was pretty scary. Who'd want to be mashed up in a dark tunnel after a good meal and plans to get screwed and all?

Anyway, Stock*head*, as I sometimes secretly called her, treated us as if we had no feelings or couldn't understand what she called the "real implications of such a tragedy." Why couldn't we? Death probably scared us more than her, especially when it happens to a young person.

She kept explaining and explaining until I had a nightmare that I was a squished princess dying in a car! I wanted to scream at Ms. Stockton to shut up, but I didn't dare. Every teacher was on "Harold Alert," so I watched my step and basically played dumb and silent.

My dad thought I might look better, or not so stupid, if I had my front teeth straightened, so I had this retainer thing I had to wear in my mouth during the day, and a whole head gear thing that hurt like hell at night. Well, the stupid thing got bent when I fell off my bike, so it wouldn't stay on my teeth and kept rattling around in my mouth.

And I must've started sucking on it without knowing it. Suddenly, out of nowhere, in the middle of one of her stupid stories, Stockhead grabs my hair and tells me only barbarians chew gum. I thought, given that it was history class and all, I'd tell her that barbarians probably didn't have Juicy Fruit, but I thought I'd better shut up. Instead, I tried to get the thing onto my teeth because when she grabbed my head it went halfway down my throat. I was choking and trying to yank my retainer up with my tongue.

Meanwhile, she was pulling my arm and leading me over to the intercom near the door. She yelled to Tarkin that I was on my way — for chewing gum. She must've thought it was quite a wad because I was almost turning blue trying to get the thing up into my mouth. I couldn't talk, even to tell her I'd go straight to the principal's office. I nodded, but she just thought I was being extra rude.

On my way to his office, I stuck about six fingers in my mouth and almost puked trying to get the thing out of my throat so I could at least talk. When I did, I just put it in my pocket because one of the wires was broken and it was cutting my mouth anyway, which is why I had it kind of moving around in the first place. I hadn't had it fixed because my dad would've killed me for breaking it. He was the one who wanted to make my mouth look better, not me. He kept telling me how expensive it was, like therapy, so I just left it like it was and I put it in in the morning so I wouldn't get yelled at.

Tarkin made me wait. He always did that. It was a technique he used on everyone to make us more nervous by the time we went in. I think he thought it would be easier to break us down and stuff if he made us wait outside his office with his fat, stuck-up secretary giving us dirty looks for an hour.

She thought she was really something because she was the principal's secretary and made sure everyone knew it, even our parents on parent night. I'll bet most of the parents didn't give a damn who she was, but she thought they did and played up the idea that she had some influence with Tarkin. I think she thought he was president of the United States or something. Really, he was just another guy who went to school to go back to school and stayed long enough to be bumped up to Principal. I bet he even knew this in a way. Maybe not. He was kind of deep into the role and all.

This seems so clear to me, but people would think I was kind of crazy if I ever talked about it. Teachers and principals are sucked up to like they control life as we know it, but they're just dweebs who couldn't be doctors or lawyers, or didn't dare try. So, they stayed in school to be aging prefects or something.

When I hear about other schools where kids ignore the teachers and tell them where to go and all, I can understand. It's just really clear to them where a lot of teachers are coming from. They're really chicken-shit and the kids know it, so they bully them. My father wouldn't have let me go to a school like that, even if there was one around, but I think I would've fit in better. In my school, it's as if teachers are terrified that we might catch on to the truth, so they act real strict and all, dressing as if they go to real jobs. I don't even think they respect themselves very much, and they're afraid we won't because in most cases they know we shouldn't.

Anyway, Tarkin said I was chewing gum and "flaunting the rules." I wasn't, but he didn't care what I said, so he suspended me again and I knew I was going to get hell from my dad and it was going to hurt my mom again. I was real upset, but tried not to show it, and then he told me I showed no remorse for my actions.

What actions? Adults always use that word. Actions. Like kids have this huge, busy conspiracy going all the time and we never sleep because we're carrying out our *actions*. What frigging actions? All I was doing was sitting there with a loose retainer cutting up my mouth, and I wasn't being responsible for my actions?

Then, because of this, look what happens. I mean, maybe it wasn't just this, but I couldn't take another sad look on my mom's face and another speech from my father about what a loser I was. I just couldn't. I mean, I'm not a winner by far, but I couldn't keep hearing it over and over. All that stuff I had to do and be to become successful in the world we keep hearing is so screwed up that no one except Donald Trump can be successful.

What's the point of suspending me and sending me home to hear more about how life sucks, I suck, and my future sucks, and how I better do all kinds of things that are never really explained to me to not suck?

I knew as I sat there that I couldn't breathe here anymore, that I couldn't just go home and say I was suspended and go through it all again. It was like I couldn't move or act anymore. Funny. Then I guess I no longer had to take responsibility for anything. I was, like, paralyzed inside and moving seemed real hard, as if I was walking through deep snow or mud or wet sand. My legs felt so heavy, it took an hour to walk home, instead of about fifteen minutes.

Tarkin had already gotten to my mom. I had never seen her look so sad and tired. She cried, but didn't say anything to me. She just looked up as I carried my knapsack into my room. I knew she was crying while she could, without crap or interference. She wouldn't be able to later when my dad got home and hit the roof. Then she'd have to stand there like his second lieutenant and nod a lot at whatever he said. My mom only cried when it was safe.

I just lay on my bed and wished I were someone famous and rich. I also wished I were dead. I knew being dead would be better than feeling so much that you start to lose feelings and then go numb all over just to live.

And I don't mean anything fancy when I talk about living. I just mean eating and going to school and coming home and sleeping and stuff. I really can say that it was after that day that I realized I should be dead, and that I'd feel better.

Or I'd *really* feel nothing and nothing would matter. I'd never get yelled at again and it wouldn't matter that no one liked me, not even my dad. I wouldn't even be Harold anymore. Harold — who the hell is that anyway? What I am inside isn't just Harold. Too bad I'd have to kill the inside too to not have to be living as Harold anymore. But that's life, at least as I see it.

I waited for my dad. He was late that night, but the waiting didn't bother me too much. If you want to know, I was thinking about where his hunting gear and ammo were. I didn't have to think too hard. He had made me get it ready tons of times when he forced me to go hunting with him. He said hunting would make a man out of me too, like the stupid private school, but he laughed his head off the first time I shot his best rifle and I flew back against a rock with the kick. But I had a few pictures in my room of when I had hit hard targets, and my dad kept one to show his friends when he was in a good mood about twice a year.

He got home around midnight. My mom and I had both waited up. We had to. He would expect us to, so that he could deal with an issue while it was still "fresh," like just gutted fish fried for breakfast on a holiday. It always felt pretty rotten to me.

To be honest, I don't even remember what he said, because I had been working at not listening anymore. He always said the same thing anyway. Then I tried to block my ears with my mind as he went at my mother. From my room, it always sounded like a hum that went up and down, louder and softer, on and on, and then was finally over just about when the sun was coming up. Then they'd go to bed and I could just imagine my mom lying there, trying not to cry, worrying, and blaming herself for all my problems while he snored like a trucker.

I just stayed awake and tried not to keep picturing my mom. I couldn't stand the thought of her all crushed inside and hurt anymore.

I fell asleep just before it was getting light, just as I had figured out how long I would have to hold my breath to die. I would have to hold it in for a long time in order to be dead. I'd no doubt just faint first and make things a hell of a lot worse because everyone would just say I was pulling a stunt.

See? They don't even know I'm not the type. I don't pull stunts or do practical jokes. I'm not the type. I don't want to because I don't find stunts funny, and I can't anyway, because everyone would read something bad into it. Cute, popular kids could do stunts and be called "wonderfully creative." If I did, it would just make me weirder and everyone would think I was stupider and crazier than ever. It wouldn't be a stunt if I ran out of oxygen and fell down.

It would be kind of a test to see how long it would take, and how it would feel to almost die and leave.

FIVE

Out of the Sun

IT WAS FINE that my dad wasn't talking to me, that he kind of pretended I didn't exist. He always did this when I'd screwed up, which was about every second day. My mom ignored me too. She didn't call me to have something to eat before school or anything because I might end up in the same room as my father and that always made her real nervous.

I didn't care because I was used to feeling nonexistent and that's all he did, pretend I wasn't there. One time, the tension was so bad for my mom, I found her in the bathroom leaning over the toilet gagging or choking or something. I mean, she was puking, but nothing was coming out. When she saw me watching her, she said she was choking on some toast.

She always pretended, and I guess that's all she knew how to do. I don't think my mom ever dared to do what was real or natural. She just kept out of everyone's way and tried to make things seem peaceful. Even when I was little, I could see what a hard job this was. I could see that she needed me to be in it with her, like it was all normal and okay. It never felt okay, though, but there was nothing I could do about it because, well, how do you make hidden things real? Or, people real? Even your own parents?

I think my dad got off on it. It was kind of a game or something and he preferred to be the guy in the game, the main man sort of, than just be himself. My mom hated it. I could tell. She'd never say so, but I could tell it was killing her in a way.

I'd say my mom kind of suffered something terrible, sort of like a crazy person who no longer knows what's real and what isn't, and has to hide and lie all the time in order to get through a day. I think my mom felt my dad would dump her like he always threatened to if she didn't fake everything and stay confused. This was his way of controlling her, so he could control his image and his phony life.

Sometimes, I didn't think it would feel too bad to kill them. It would be mercy killing for my mom, and for my dad, well, kind of a reality test. How would he be with a gun in his face, no choices, and nothing great to quote? I never planned to find out.

The sun was too bright. My eyes always hurt in the light and I wore sunglasses a lot because I got headaches from too much light. The florescent lights at school gave me a headache in about four seconds, but I wasn't allowed to wear tinted glasses there. I always had to take them off and squint to try not to feel too sick.

The basement window had this spotlight of sun shining in as I opened the old wooden chest where my dad kept all his shiny handguns. He had so many it was as if he thought he was from the Wild West or something.

I loaded three .38s right then and there and stuck them in the back of my pants. Next, I think I put a million bullets in my dad's ammo belt. I closed the chest real quiet and then went to where I kept the sports stuff my dad bought me and took my special .22 automatic out of its sheath.

It was still as clean as flossed and brushed teeth from when I cleaned it the last time. It was a Reuger — a real beauty — and I loaded it and jammed more ammo into my pants. I cocked it a few times as quietly as I could because where I was kneeling was right under the kitchen where they were sitting, eating cereal and listening to the news on the radio. They did this every morning like robots, without saying a word to each other, as if they were getting silent, coded instructions for a CIA assignment or something.

I could've died in my sleep and they would never know because they were in their breakfast trance. Anyway, I didn't care. I might have cared before or something, but I don't know. I just made sure I had enough ammo to blow a whole mountain away. Seemed like I was ready for a big kill of some kind.

I think I only paused for a minute. My rifle felt heavy and cold, like it had been in a fridge or something. I was wondering how it could be so cold all by itself. Then I heard a chair scrape on the floor upstairs and I froze for a moment behind the furnace, waiting. I didn't know if someone would come down.

If so, it'd probably be my dad, but I hoped no one would. I didn't want to be caught with my dad's guns and my rifle and all this ammo as if I was going to start a war or something. I didn't know what I'd say, and I knew I wouldn't shoot him. I'd just take some more shit and put everything away as he yelled at me because I was hanging out in the basement instead of getting ready for school.

I was allowed to go to school again because my dad phoned and made this great deal that got me two months of detentions instead. I'd be right back where I started and I couldn't remember where that was anymore, so I was more scared than ever.

I didn't know where to go back to, or how, like I was walking in my sleep, in a bad dream or something, and I'd never wake up. I'd never be awake or alive again to do the messing up and faking and sometimes just being left alone for a day, which I liked. It was kind of like before I'd even done anything or anything had changed, everything was already different and strange, and my life as it was, was already over. I felt real scared by that because it felt sort of supernatural or something. But I felt more scared that I would be caught where I was. I'd be worse than nowhere.

For at least five minutes, which felt like a million years, I leaned against the furnace and shook like crazy. I put my face against the warm metal and thought it might steady me, but it just made me feel more scared, sort of confused or crazy, so I moved away and just knelt for a moment a few feet from the stairs. I watched the top landing and tried not to breathe too loudly. It was like a stage in a play, set up and waiting for a scene to happen, or sort of like a scary movie on pause with no rewind.

My heart beat so hard and fast that I could barely breathe. It was like it was the only thing that was real and it was screaming at me to stop and stay in this scary nowhere place. But when no one came, I kept moving. I don't know how, but I moved slowly, taking each step like it was half a mountain.

My hands were sweaty and I almost dropped the rifle as I squeezed real hard to grip the railing with my other hand. I had to stop because my eyes stung with acid sweat dripping from my scalp and dirty hair. I couldn't see clearly.

Even as I reached the top step and the door, everything was blurred and darkish like someone had turned some weird, dim kind of light on. I came through the door and turned toward the kitchen and just stood there, half facing them, with the rifle hanging at my hidden side. My breathing was loud enough for them to hear even over the sports news that my dad always made everyone shut up for. But they didn't move or look.

Then I turned to face them dead on and, after I moved, my dad turned to me and looked real calm, but mad. He saw the gun at my side, not aimed or anything, but I had it and was just standing there when I was supposed to be ready for school. He was about to yell at me when my mom looked up and jumped out of her chair so fast it tipped over and she spilled coffee all over the table onto my father's lap. He looked away from me and at her as if she was an idiot, overreacting and all. As he was grabbing a napkin to clean his pants, I looked into my mom's eyes and raised the gun.

I'll never forget the way she looked. She looked more sad than scared, sort of like she always expected me to kill them, and as if she wanted to say sorry or something, like she deserved it. I had to not look to pull the trigger, so I aimed and closed my eyes and shot my mom right in the neck.

I would've puked right then and there because I blew her head off, and half her body sprayed all over the kitchen, but I stayed in nowhere and my dad came at me with a look in his eyes and a growling sound that made it easy to shove the gun at him as he dove at me to grab it.

Even after his chest kind of exploded and he flew back onto the table, he had that look. He looked like a savage animal would look, real scary — a killer that had had an opportunity to kill, but missed. It was sort of like this was our moment and he would show me who was the killer, but he got his heart and guts shot out before he could get me.

Maybe he was surprised, but he seemed more ready to fight than surprised. Even with my mom's scream, and my dad's growl and attack, it all seemed, well, kind of normal or expected.

It's strange. Even though I was kind of sick right after because of the excitement and all, it didn't seem like anything really weird had happened or that anything was wrong.

Only thing was that I was covered with my dad's guts and the whole kitchen and half the hall were a bloody mess. Funny, that's what my dad used to call our house even when it was perfect — a bloody mess! Then my mom would set about cleaning it all over again, pretending she agreed with him and was real sorry.

I was glad my mom couldn't see the mess, even though I wondered whether I should clean it up to be proper like. I wished my dad could've seen it and had a fit, a real one, over a *real* mess. Hot blood, guts, brains and coffee spilled all over the floor. He'd freak, for sure.

But instead he just lay arched over the kitchen table in a bloody sweat suit with his face frozen in rage. He looked ridiculous, like a bloody turtle, dead on its back after having tried to win a fight with a rabid wolf. Stupid ass. I don't know whose blood it was I could hear gushing onto the floor like an open tap. But it wasn't loud enough to keep me from hearing the phony, cheerful jerk on the radio promising a sunny and terrific day for the fun-loving, hardworking, good folk of our nowhere little town. Just another sunny day. Nothing new.

I didn't usually take a shower before school, but there was no way I could even answer the door looking like I did. It looked like I had been shot and beaten up and smashed around more than them. I'm not sure I thought of it then, but I must've known no one would find them for as long as I needed, or at all unless I told someone, because they didn't have anyone who would check on them.

My dad did the consulting stuff with the school board and my mom was just subbing this term and she didn't have to go in. Plus, they didn't have any friends who would check on them for no reason or just come over. They'd probably lie there 'til the New Year. Come to think of it, I guess it would've been weird going home after school that night. They would've been less likely to notice me than ever, but I'd sure notice *them*. I couldn't avoid them.

And they'd probably be so real as dead people I'd want to study them. I'm sure I couldn't have faked doing my homework like always and just worked around them. I didn't even know where I was going.

Funny, they were dead, but I didn't feel like they were. I was just sort of like a robot hanging out. At the time, I wasn't thinking about anything other than getting all that stuff off me. Now, I wonder what I would've done if the other stuff hadn't happened. I wonder if I would've hid them or something and pretended they left. Stupid as the cops are, they still would've known and I'd be in the same place I'm in now, only maybe not quite as bad.

I was late for school by the time I washed up. I didn't care. I pulled the curtains in the living room and cleaned the outside of my rifle so it still shone. It smelled so strong from being shot, I kept coughing all the way to the garage to find something to wrap it in that didn't look too obvious. I found an old limp, canvas golf bag of my dad's and stuck the rifle in barrel first. Then I put some of the ammo in the pockets and slung it over my shoulder before closing the garage door and walking to the back of the house. I took the long way, through the woods, but I was definitely going to school.

I crouched in the brush by the track field for a while. I tried to figure out how to get to the side where there was a parking lot and a small hill I could lie on and, from there, look down on the play area. I still didn't know what would actually happen, but I had a powerful feeling for the first time since I went to the nowhere place.

I felt excited by how I was going to scare the shit out of some asshole kids who everyone thought were so great because they got good marks, or had girlfriends and boyfriends, or were good at sports. It gave me a hard-on to imagine everyone's faces all twisted up in terror — all confused and lost and totally messed up in the head because something was happening they couldn't control and never planned.

I didn't feel like I was nowhere and no one – not even the skinny kid, Harold. I felt more like an important force, something coming, an act of nature like an earthquake or tornado that hits and pulls people out of their little mean habits and makes them pay attention to their every move, even their breathing.

Just like my parents now, only different at the same time, all these people would have to be real, even for just a few seconds, if I made them think they might be dead soon.

With Tarkin, I thought I'd aim right at his balls, because he doesn't have any, and make him crawl on his knees in circles until he started to blubber and beg like a little baby. I'd make him wait and wait before I decided what to do and show him how it feels to be treated like a turd, to be kept waiting when you're scared. I'd show him for sure.

I snuck back and around to get to the edge of the lot that led up to the hill. I climbed it and waited. The gun was loaded and I was kind of leaning toward doing something that would blow everything apart, but I stopped thinking. I wasn't thinking about who I'd get and why anymore, not even Tarkin. I was just moving, crawling and pushing my body into the hill as if I could disappear into it.

I remember being cold, right to the bone, as if I were dead, but watching myself and feeling death in myself at the same time. I can't describe it any better than that. For a split second, while I was lying there on my side with my head down in the dirt, I felt like crying.

Something jumped up from my stomach and chest into my head that almost made me scream like a baby or something, but I stopped it real fast. I was real scared by it, the feeling that is. It felt like if I'd let it happen, let the feeling get bigger, I would drown in it, die in it, because it was much stronger than me and from a place I didn't know about. It felt like an alien was trying to take me down and kill me with feelings. It scared me more than anything I'd ever felt.

Looking up and thinking about going forward seemed easy compared to letting it get me. I knew I could lie there and die in that stuff in my gut or I could keep going, not think, and push the feeling back. I wasn't even thinking 'bout what I'd

already done, that I'd just offed my parents. I didn't think about
that until much later. In fact, at first, when I was told and
accused of killing them, I didn't even believe it. Again, I wondered what part of me had the guts.

Before I really knew what I was doing, I was kind of march-
ing, like a soldier during drill or something, down the hill to
the schoolyard. There were a few kids there, younger ones,
and they didn't see me at first and when they did, they just
kind of pointed and laughed. They even saw the gun, but they
thought it was funny, like I thought I was a big shot or something for carrying it.

It was the first time I felt nothing when they laughed at
me. I just walked right past them, about fifteen feet from them,
and went in the side door closest to the cafeteria and furthest
from the office. This was pretty smart, but I didn't really think
about it. The door was just there and it was the first lunch
hour, so it was real good timing.

I remember a bit about moving along the hallway, sideways, with my back against the wall, and the gun raised alertly
like a guy on a SWAT team. I kept thinking someone would
come along, even though I didn't think about what I'd do to
them or anything.

I was just sort of surprised to get all the way to the cafeteria, which was full of assholes and cool kids and guys and girls
faking like they were married or engaged or something, and
then I was inside. A few people saw me right away. A few
started to smile and mock me. Almost instantly, though, they
weren't smiling anymore and started screaming.

I swear that was before anything had even happened. And
then I just started shooting and shooting and popping people
and moving through bunches of running and ducking kids,
shooting as many as I could. I never heard such a sound.

Banging furniture and screams from guys and girls that
sounded wild, like terrified animals you see running from hunt-
ers shooting at them from jeeps on TV documentaries.

Some were screaming on the floor behind and beside me and I kept moving and I got a big guy that was a football hero or something. I was still shooting when some guy jumped on my back and knocked me sideways, and then another guy helped him. I remember seeing the first guy's gut was shot in and I could feel his hot blood on my arms and neck.

There were about ten guys on me and kids were screaming, "A shooter! A shooter!" like idiots. It sounded like, "The sky is falling! The sky is falling!" like they didn't really believe it, but were screaming something to get it to stop.

I wriggled away as a few teachers started calling kids out of the cafeteria. I crawled under tables and chairs to a window some girl had smashed to get out, pulling me and my rifle out as someone yelled, "There he goes! He's over there!"

I got out and ran as fast as I could to my place on the hill. I guess I thought there was a magic place there where they couldn't find me, and I could stay there for a while and they would've learned their lesson. I'd wash up and go to school tomorrow as myself and listen to what people said about the shooter and all.

I wasn't even scared, just kind of interested when about a million police cars and ambulances and fire trucks came racing into the schoolyard with all their sirens going. I lay on the hill and watched kids coming out crying. Some had blood on them.

A few teachers were running around in circles as if they were doing something important. I like how they were there now that it was finished. Just running around – running to the police, running to each other like they had a special pact that didn't include the kids. About ten just ran for their cars and took off while other kids were crying and running across the road to the other side to make sure they were away from the school, and me.

It was a real mess, a real one, not like someone sprayed graffiti on a wall and we had to have an assembly to discuss how serious it was, and how it was anarchy and all and those who did it should turn themselves in.

It was really something, like the sky *had* fallen in a way and no one, not even the smart-ass teachers, knew what to do. Even the cops looked sort of scrambled and disorganized. It was real satisfying to watch everyone so screwed up and knowing nothing about anything but not wanting to die. I must've known they'd find me too. I must've because some kids saw me go through the window.

The hill still felt like a place where, if I stayed still, I'd be invisible. I was there for what seemed like hours, just lying there with my rifle, real fascinated by the show. First time I'd ever seen anything go on at that school that wasn't bullshit. Even the teachers' running to save their own skin wasn't bullshit. It was real, and I'd seen it before in my mind. I didn't expect to see any teachers be heroes. I already knew better— that was the point.

While I was still trying to shoot, some macho guy had twisted my arm behind my back and it started to ache, so I went back the way I came and sat against a tree in the woods halfway back to my home.

Another guy's blood was still on me, getting sticky and all, and it was making me a bit nervous. I couldn't stand it on me. It even had a smell and it made me feel a bit crazy again, like on the hill, and I tried to scratch it off me so hard that I cut myself in long stripes with my own nails. Then I had his blood and mine mixing together and I rubbed up against a tree and used some leaves to try to get it off.

I wished I had a blanket, even a pillow. I was so tired, I don't even remember falling asleep. I didn't know it was possible to sleep being so cold and all. It was as if the trees had never had any sun shone on them at all and were still cold from the Stone Age or something. I was shaking, more like jerking. Must've been some kind of reaction, as my mom would say.

It's kind of obvious that they found me. I was sort of doz-ing when a huge dog, like a wolf, jumped me and a cop came and held me down with the dog.

He was yelling, "Suspect apprehended! Suspect appre-hended!" into a walkie-talkie. He was all out of breath as if I'd fought him off with a machete or something. I was just lying there like a log and he acted like he had just captured a team of bank robbers in mid-air while parachuting or something.

He just jumped on top of a kid and pressed a heavy, black bat into his throat 'til the kid choked and his neck cracked. Big man! He threw his whole body into it and I thought I was going to get decapitated.

You know what happened next and all. I was cuffed and sort of pushed and dragged to one of the cop cars. I could barely see because of all the lights flashing and cops shining these really bright flashlights in my face. I think they just wanted to see that I looked like hell.

There were kids and parents standing around crying and yelling and hugging, and they tried to push forward when three cops brought me into the schoolyard to one of the cars. All I could see were mouths and teeth, no actual faces or even eyes.

A million angry mouths were moving fast, in weird, bent shapes, and with lips all puckering up and out, as if they were fleshy gun barrels trying to spit bullets at me. Their lips stuck out like wet rubber — full of hate, and then I'd see bared teeth like a shark's, then the "shoot 'im dead" pucker thing again.

I thought then that I must be dreaming or something. They weren't like real people — you know, slow moving, po-lite, and kind of indifferent to everything, especially me. These folk had gone mental and wanted to kill me. I could feel that on top of what I'd done, I had made them more angry and scared than they had ever been.

I was kind of glad to get into the car, even though I knew the two cops might throw me off a cliff or something. I could tell they hated me, but I knew I had a better chance with them than with the killer mouths.

Funny, I always felt shot by what people said, but I never noticed how their mouths actually looked like the barrel of a gun before. All that was different was that these noisy people were making their feelings real clear. They didn't just hate me, or talk about me behind my back, or not give a damn.

They wanted me dead, gone, after a good, long torture. I had messed up their lives and blown away some of the "good guys," some of whom were real assholes and real mean themselves, but could never have done what I did. People are okay with, even used to others doing, weird, terrible things as a kind of way of life. It's the *big*, mean things that get you locked up or killed, unless you're the government killing people in another country or something.

I wanted the car to get going, but one cop kept radioing the chief's office and the jail. Then we sat there while they radioed the other cops in the area to say that they were on their way and that they had what they called an ETA of about fifteen minutes. It was real scary waiting.

I knew I couldn't get out because there were no door handles in the back and no way to open the windows either. Plus, I was cuffed and locked away from the cops by the steel mesh stuff for dogs. I was afraid because the mouths were getting closer and I thought they might break into the car and get me. Who could blame them? I stayed pretty still and finally, they took me away.

From then on, 'til now, you pretty well know what happened. It was gross, but much less gross than what would've happened if the cops had wasted more time, or not put me into the car. I would've been pulverized, especially by the parents who came out of nowhere. They would've smashed me dead, like they were just driving over road kill. They'd be so excited to kill me, but it'd just be a slight jerk and bump on their way home.

SIX

Dead and Alive

SHE WON'T LEAVE. I can't believe Jessica's hanging around here instead of going back to school. I wish she hadn't come home at all. What was the point, other than to arrange a funeral? I don't mean to be disrespectful, but anyone could've done that.

Worse, she wanted to see me. I sure didn't want to see her, but they let her in and made me come to the visiting area. I couldn't look at her because it made me think of what I did.

I mean, it's not as if I don't know, but I could pretend that I didn't, and that my mom and dad were just somewhere pissed off at me and ignoring me as usual because I had finally really screwed up. When I see my sister, though, all sad and pale and looking at me like she wants to cry, it makes me feel crazy inside.

She's missing tests and all kinds of important stuff and she said that she's having her clothes sent back so that she can be here. I freaked out when she told me because I couldn't imagine why she would want to come back to such a, well, messy situation.

I almost croaked when she said that she wanted to be here partly because I'm here. Why would she say that? Is she temporarily insane or something? I mean, she had to do everything with a lawyer about my parents' investments and stuff and answer a million questions about me. She says she still wants to stay close like a brother and sister! She told me I was all she had left in the way of family, as if some maniac broke into our house and killed our parents.

I did it! I told her that, as if she didn't know, again and again, and she just nodded her head and said "I know" in a real soft voice, as if by saying it softly enough, it wouldn't be real. It was almost as if she didn't believe me or something, or as if maybe I knew the guys who did it and somehow it was only indirectly my fault, but not really, if you know what I mean.

People, the guards, that is, say I act kind of strange. Well, she's acting like I did something good, or nothing at all, and am in prison by mistake or something. As my dad would say, talk about out of touch with reality!

To tell you the truth, I never figured this part. I never thought my sister would act this way. I didn't think about her at all — or my parents for that matter — but if I had, I would've thought she'd come home, have a funeral or something, sell our house, get some bucks and go back to school.

But she's here. *Staying* here. What frigging kind of life is she going to have now? She's the monster's sister! I wish I'd asked her before I did it. Stupid thought because of course, I wouldn't or couldn't. But if I'd known what she would do with her life because of what I did, I wouldn't have done it. Just for her, somehow, I wouldn't have done it.

I would've found *any way* to stop myself. I would've just burned a house or something, and smashed my dad's car and then killed myself. I never would've done this to her. She knew me. She never once ignored me like I was wasn't real. Maybe

you can help her. I'm dead, but maybe you can help my sister.
I wish I could help her, but she doesn't really get it, or me anymore, or what I did, or something. *Something's* out of whack.

In the middle of all this, when I was real upset and all
about my sister, my lawyer came in. His name is Robert Spencer, but he says to call him Bob. He's pretending to be kind of
into my case, even though it's obvious he's kind of nervous
around me and doesn't want to be my lawyer.

He's telling me I have to be real careful about what I say.
Even to you. He told me that he has listened to my tapes, and
that really upsets me. I'm really mad at you for that! You told
me only you would listen to them. And now I find out that
some "super cool" guy with a movie star haircut hiding his
bald spot, and a gold pen he plays with a lot, has been listening to me when I was almost crying and all. I wouldn't have
said anything if I'd known!

He told me he made you do it. You two must have a thing
or something. Either he's covering for you or you're both just
assholes for not telling me what was going on. He said I might
say something on tape that would affect my trial and that you
might lose the tapes or something. Does he think you're stupid? *Are* you stupid?

To tell you the truth, I wouldn't want you to be stupid,
but I don't want you to mess with me either. I feel you might
have messed with me by letting Spencer hear me telling you
stuff. I should tell you to take off and leave me alone.

This sucks, because I actually need to ask you if you could
come in and see me for longer this time. I don't want to just
send tapes to you through the guards who I bet listen to them
too.

I need to talk to you about my trial. I've been here so
long that I haven't thought much about a trial. I mean, I did
it, right? So, what will happen at a trial? And then what will
happen once they say at a trial that I did it. Where will I go? I
need to talk to you here, in person, before I can talk anymore

like this. I want you to tell them to leave me here, at the county jail.

It's bad, but I know how bad, and I pretty well have a handle on it. That lawyer guy who someone just appointed to do my trial said I'll be moved. Moved where? He said it depended on when my case "came to trial." He said even though I'm not sixteen, I'll go to a worse place because I'll probably be tried as an adult. He had a real serious look on his face when he said that, like it was a death sentence or something.

I'm real scared and I was just starting to feel I could stand it here. I don't miss school. I don't even miss my room where I spent my whole life. I just miss my sister because I wrecked her life and because she might need me. God, is that weird! She might need me and I killed our parents, *her* parents. You'd think she'd sneak in and murder me when no one was looking. I would if I were her.

I'm getting real nervous and doing that gagging thing again. I'm asking the guard to call you, okay? Can you please come to see me here? I mean, really, be here as soon as possible? I think I might lose it.

⊰⊱⊰⊱

I just puked and I think I'm going to shit my pants. It hasn't happened since they brought me in. I have to tell you I'm sort of counting on you coming. I won't beg, or maybe I will, but it's real urgent that you come or I'm going to puke and crap myself down to nothing. Talk to Spencer if it'll help. But come even if he says no, okay?

⊰⊱⊰⊱

I'm sorry that the tape stopped twice just then. I sort of panicked a little. I didn't want you to hear everything that's going on with me, like body stuff.

I was going to say we could maybe have like a real session, unless that's strictly forbidden. I could try to get some money to pay you for your time, but we'd say it was just a visit anyway. I hate asking anyone for anything, and you're not even the really sucky type who would make it easy, but I have to talk to someone, and you're the only one I've talked to since I was caught or whatever. In fact, even before that, there was no one I talked to at all.

So, now that I feel like things are going to change for me again, I'm kind of reaching out, as my old counselor used to tell me to do. But I didn't then. So, this is my first time and, to be honest, it doesn't feel real good, that's for sure.

You see, when it was just me, and all I had to do was stay here and rot into a mental case, I sort of didn't think about much — especially about what happened. I tried not to wonder what was going on outside of here about me — I mean with people hating me and wanting to burn me alive and everything. But then my sister comes and acts all weird like nothing's wrong, and Spencer comes and talks about what they're going to do with me, just like my dad, and I'm freaked out. Why don't they just leave me alone and let me just hang out here?

There's a day room here and I get two hours of TV a day if I don't cause any trouble. And the food's sort of okay. There's a different kind of tension here than at home. Some days the guards are tense, or someone other than myself has a bad day and freaks out and we all get kind of uptight. It's not too bad, though, and I could sort of do it here. Life, I mean.

It's even easier than out there, whether I screw up or not. Things are pretty clear here, and I like that. It's the first time in my life I kind of know what I'm supposed to do and all. I even know how to get the odd privilege, something I've never had in my life, at home or at school. I never understood how to earn one. I was always sort of too concentrated on not being destructive, or an idiot, or getting my mom in trouble because I tracked dirt in the house on my shoes or something.

The last few days we watched War TV. That's what we call it — the War Channel. We watched Baghdad and some other areas over there getting the shit kicked out of them at night. There was this cool lady with an accent reporting it kind of like a fair reporting of a soccer game. We also watched what an older guy two cells down called a "systemic *coup d'état*" going on in the House of Representatives.

They're impeaching Clinton for sucking boobs, getting a blow job and then saying he didn't. I wouldn't admit that to anyone, even a friend if I had one. I'd be so embarrassed. It would be harder to admit if I never actually, like, had the full thing with her, if you know what I mean. Would *you*?

I mean, I know you wouldn't be unfaithful to your husband or anything, nor would I think you'd suck boobs or get a blow job, but if you did something else, as a woman, would you go to your professional group or whatever and admit it? If they asked you, would you tell them right away and include every little detail? I bet not.

I'm sure glad I'm not Clinton. What a great job to have taken from you by a bunch of assholes who probably blow each other off in the cloakroom and stuff. Anyway, we got to watch it all on television, the president turning all gray and old-looking, and the green glow of bombs and anti-aircraft fire in Iraq. It was far out. Did you watch it? Watching War TV is an example of a privilege here.

I was thinking later that it was sort of like how all the cameras gathered around my school after I shot up the cafeteria. Two of the guards kept telling me that I had turned the town into a "media circus" because everyone from around the world wanted to come here and see dead kids and the place where it happened. He told me they all wanted to see me too.

I can believe that. On the day they wrestled me to the ground when I was sleeping, I was soon caught right in the face by all these cameras and stuff. I didn't even turn away. I smiled at one guy from the back of the cop car, and I heard him say to his talking TV friend that I was psycho.

Just because I was smiling, I'm psycho? I mean, I wouldn't smile *now*, but it was like a nervous reaction or something. They would've been disappointed if I'd hidden my head, which is what I'd know to do now. Funny, you have to have committed a few big, dramatic crimes to learn how and where to put your head for the cameras and stuff — especially when it's entertainment and somewhere people are watching, eating their macaroni and cheese, and yelling at someone to answer the phone.

You could learn to kill by just watching all the stuff on TV, but someone could probably give workshops on how to handle yourself for the cameras after you do it. I mean, I can see doing it for the attention and all because you sure get it. To make the most of it, even to affect what they call public opinion, you could watch every move you make and maybe make a bundle later with a good story. But you'd have to make sure you get the story ready before a trial because once you're found guilty, you're not allowed to make money and stuff.

You'd really have to have a plan, almost a "kill to get famous plan," to do it right. Maybe even hire someone ahead of time — someone who wouldn't tell — and then start the action. Then, like that Ollie North, the soldier guy who hid money and sold arms to international bad guys, and tons of others who got in trouble with the law, you'd get your own radio show, be on Larry King, maybe even get to run for politics. But, for politics, it's better to be a wrestler.

As I said, it's easier in here — plainer or something. At least I knew we were watching a war. Pretty colors have never impressed me. I knew there was lots of blood under all that lime green and yellow light that looked like fireworks for a ballet or something.

It's funny how we train and get all patriotic about expert

killers on our side who are always "directed by God" and stuff. Everyone else is killing and fighting back as a force of evil. I guess I'm a force of evil. I kind of don't have a parent around to tell people I'm misunderstood and to make up great stories about how sensitive and helpful I can be.

Remember that Goldman guy who made sure his son, who O.J. Simpson killed, was known as a nice guy? Meanwhile, O.J. spent lots of money to have screwed up, racist heads screwed around even more to get off. At least, that's how I see it.

Then, O.J. got to pretend to write a book and make a set of videos to sell because he murdered two people, as long as he did it during the trial in case he was found guilty, which he most certainly was, but wasn't. Just goes to show you that sometimes even guilty people get away with stuff by doing something even worse.

You can see there isn't much to do here but think. And it's not all 'bout how crazy everything is, or about what's on TV. You think about other, meaner guys here and how you have to try to stay on top of things and out of their way. And, you always wonder what's next in the way of a bad surprise or, in my case, about what's going to happen to me because of a trial or something.

Some of the guys in here who I see in the day room think about their wives and kids. Some are waiting to be sent somewhere too, and they wonder where and for how long. We all, in our way, wonder and wander in our minds. Lots of the guys think and talk about sex a lot too. Real gross.

I don't, if you want to know. I don't want you to come to see me like I need female company or something. As I said, I just really need to talk to someone from the outside now because that's where all the decisions will come from. Especially because they're based on discussions and emotions and motions from the outside where things are crazy and complex and no one knows the whole truth.

You're the only one who can fill me in, and the only one who stepped in to listen, for whatever reason. I don't even care why. You might be smart-crazy too, and just using me, but you're all I've got, which is pathetic but true, and okay with me.

I'm waiting to hear, and I'm being real good so they'll tell me and not accidentally on purpose screw up your visit if you decide to come, which, as you can tell by my going on and on about it, I hope you do. I'd give up TV privileges for three months just to talk to you once.

And I know and am surer about TV than I am about you any day. Priorities sure get screwed up in here. I never asked or hoped for anything before. I never would've. I didn't need to 'til I managed to screw up my already useless life.

I also know that in addition to being pretty pathetic and all about making it known that I need to see you, that I won't try anymore if you don't come. I'm not threatening or anything, I just wouldn't have any reason to try to do things right here.

It's mostly with the guards that I try not to get in the way or make a mistake. The inmates are harder to figure out and it's kind of unpredictable as to how to stay in their good books. In fact, they don't have good books, just moods. Everyone's real aware of moods in here, as well as of the goings-on with others, even though you pretend you don't know anything.

You have to know who to stay away from, even in the shower if something went wrong for some guy that day. One guy's wife wasn't allowed to visit last week and he punched out an older guy here 'til you couldn't tell which part of his face was what.

Part of what's kind of strange here is that even if you're the one who gets beaten up, you lose privileges or get punished. That doesn't mean it's not clear or plain, it's just how it is. And I know enough now to just let myself get into it with my eyes open.

If I decided to, maybe I could even get my head bashed in so I *really* don't feel anymore, and wouldn't need to see you or get information or anything. I'd probably need to get my heart bashed in too, though. I wouldn't want to be able to feel but not think, or think but not feel, at least without having control over it.

I've always tried to control those two things about me, and it's come in handy here. It's just when things get really hyped up and someone screams all night and the guards march through and bang on our cells and call us names and stuff, I can't stand it.

Also, I hear the "killer kid" more than twenty times a day and sometimes, I get a bit crazy and I can't control everything inside me. I definitely need to control my insides. If I don't, I remember every face that ever looked at me like I was puke. I think of the teachers who used to laugh at me, my dad being ashamed of me, my mom crying, and how I couldn't save her and all sorts of stuff.

I know you're wondering if I think of that day, and I wish you weren't. I wish I didn't know you were because I try not to. Even though I don't have much control over that matter, it only comes to me in flashes, and I can't breathe for a few seconds, and then it goes away. I never know when it might come — the flash — and I try not to wait for it or wonder when it will come. If I do, I might make it come more often or for longer. The worst flash is my mom's face, knowing. I think I relieved her, like she always knew it was coming or something.

With the kids I shot, if you want to know, so far all I remember is them laughing at me and then all of a sudden screaming bloody murder like squealing little pigs. Happy, mocking little jackasses screaming, and then falling into mommy's arms, and police running all over the place wondering what could possibly go so wrong in a schoolyard.

Now, the kids at school are all as screwed up as I am, all lost and sick in the world and all. They're still all being lied to by stupid, stunned, cowardly, messed up adults who are scared of kids like me who are different, or who don't turn out right, even in the thinking of their own parents.

They're all being told that I'm gone now, that everything's alright, that I'll never come back and all, and they don't have to worry — especially if a judge says to fry me or inject me with poison, which parents don't want because I wouldn't suffer enough.

But you know what? The kids know. Or, most do. They're a bit like me, and know more than any stupid adult that something about what happened was "perfectly normal under the circumstances," as adults say about a lot of things. Even the dumb, adorable, super-cool kids will be less adorable and cool now.

This kind of stuff makes them real nervous when they thought they had a handle on everything. Their perfect, pretty lives will never be the same either! So much for living!

Please don't think I should wipe this smile off my face because I'm not smiling. Just because they're not smiling now doesn't mean I can, for sure. I only had that one time of power. So, as I tried to say, I'm asking in a really intense way for you to consider coming in here to see me.

It's not true — what they say about "it can't hurt to try." It can, too, asking like this. It hurts more than stupid adults ever try to understand. Try, try, and never cry.

Well, I didn't and I'm not crying now either. But please come. We could keep it short and have a calm time talking. Just so you know, I'm waiting every minute to hear.

SEVEN

Darkening Light

"YOU'RE DOING WHAT I CAN'T STAND shrinks doing. I mean I'm real grateful that you came and all, but can't you talk to me without me having to spell everything out for you?"

"Why don't you sit down, Harold?" Dr. Rosenthal leaned forward from her prison issue metal chair, halfway across the cell. Harold was walking in circles, first one way, and then the other. His sneakers were squeaking on the cement floor. The shrill, moaning sound of his rubber soles befitted Harold's agitated exterior.

"Harold, sit down."

Harold defied Dr. Rosenthal by making two more circles before plunking himself down on his cot. He didn't look at her. He stared at his hands, fingers clenched white, in a double fist hanging between his knees.

"Harold? Harold!" She paused. "You've got to talk to me. You called me here, and I believe you need to talk to me, but you have to do it, or I'll walk."

"Good for you!" he said sarcastically. "Must be nice! I can't do anything but spin in circles in this little cave I'm in!"

He threw himself down on the bed, folded his arms over his forehead, and stared with cold anger at the cracked, multi-stained ceiling.

"And who's fault is that, Harold?" Harold didn't seem to hear the question. "Harold? Whose fault is it?"

After turning his head toward the wall, he whispered, "I *don't know*! The world's!"

"The world's? Why is it the world's fault, Harold? Tell me why."

"Cause it sucks! Cause it hurts to live every damn day. No one notices or cares, and they never will! No one gives a damn how much it hurts us!"

"Who's 'us', Harold?" Dr. Rosenthal asked, leaning back against the hard, unwelcoming chair.

Harold looked furious, frustrated, as if he might yell or even lunge at Dr. Rosenthal. She remained still, steady, waiting for his reply.

"Us! You know, those of us who don't mean anything to anyone, or to the whole screwed up world either! Those of us who can't be cool or a super athlete or screw girls, or who don't look right . . . whatever! That's who!"

Dr. Rosenthal shifted slightly in her chair. She wanted Harold to express himself, but she also wanted to get to why he wanted to see her. She was on a schedule and didn't have much time. She was thinking about how ironic this was. No time for Harold, to let him vent and then to work cautiously to bring him out further than he had come thus far with the safe distance provided by technology.

He was right. There was never enough time to really tend to most people's deepest, driving needs and feelings. Most people in pain or trouble are afraid enough of their own feelings, what they tell *themselves*, let alone of what they share with others. Plus, she thought with a sigh, here was a boy who was long lost, not just in immediate and serious trouble.

She wasn't proud of the fact that she felt like leaving.

She wasn't sure she had it in her to pull him out, to fight him or to try to tame him with kindness. This boy didn't trust the sun and the moon, let alone her, or any other adult. The only reason she stayed, at this point, was that she felt he was *trying* to trust her, someone. In addition, she had something she had to tell him and the sooner the better.

She sighed and pressed her fingers into her forehead. "Harold? You need to tell me. Now. You have to find a way to tell me why you needed to see me in person today, okay?" She removed her hand from her head and lay it open on her knee.

Harold brought his hands to his face and then rubbed both sides of his head roughly, as if he were scrubbing dirt away, or waking himself up.

"I'm hearing things . . . and I'm scared." He was still looking to the side of his cell as if he hoped she wouldn't hear if he didn't make eye contact.

"Hearing what? What kinds of things? And from where, Harold?" Dr. Rosenthal thought maybe he was hearing voices or getting messages in dreams, in which case it would make a huge difference in how he should be handled. She'd want to tell Spencer. It could change the defense strategy.

"Well, from around here, but also from my 'I don't give a shit' lawyer."

Realizing Harold was referring to things he was hearing from other people, she shifted gears to listen. "What are you hearing?"

"Well, first of all, I'm hearing that you're not really my shrink 'n all. That this is just a short-term study or something, and that you're telling my lawyer everything. That's one thing I heard that really burned me up. You tricked me just like everyone else! I should've known I was right when I thought you'd crap out on me!"

"I didn't trick you, Harold. I have spent a great deal of time, both personally and professionally, trying to understand you, trying to figure out how best to help you, and to give you a way to talk about what you needed or wanted to share about your life." She paused to judge his reaction. What she was saying was true, but part of what he felt was also valid. "It wasn't a trick. Treatment, per se, can't start until after your trial if the court orders it.

"At first, I didn't know this. That's my fault, but you did need someone to talk with, especially at the beginning when you wouldn't talk, remember? Then, when you worked so well with the tapes, well, we just kept going. They have helped me to understand you, and I know they've helped you too. You've even said as much on one or two of them. I wanted to help you to release some feelings, so I asked the permission of the DA and your lawyer. But it wasn't a trick by any stretch of the imagination and I *do not* share *everything* with *anyone!*"

Harold swung his head abruptly and faced the woman head-on. "Yeah, but you *are* sharing some stuff and I was talking to *you* — not every jackass who wants a little listen to what the monster kid says! And *not* my asshole lawyer!"

Dr. Rosenthal rubbed her forehead again, this time with the three middle fingers of both hands. "Harold, I guard those tapes very carefully. You bet I have colleagues who would just love to listen to them, but I lock them away. And for your information, I think about what you have shared with me on those tapes everyday. I feel I know you and that is very, very precious to me! I wouldn't let a soul listen to those tapes, except for certain parts that might be helpful or harmful."

Harold sneered. "They were so precious to you! Yeah? Well, what about Spencer? Why didn't you *tell* me he would listen to parts of them?"

"Fair enough. I don't blame you, Harold, and I understand that you feel tricked in that way. To be honest with you, when I came in that first night, and then the next day, I didn't know that there was not going to be any, ah, formal therapy, or help for you until after you were tried.

"I found out two weeks into our taping sessions when

your lawyer called and said we would have to stop. Well, I argued and negotiated and badgered the poor guy until we came to an agreement. The only way I, or we, Harold, could continue was if I let him listen to certain parts of your story that might affect your case. I signed a document swearing an oath of secrecy. He hasn't heard much of the really personal stuff."

"*What case?!*" Harold interrupted. "What's he going to argue, that the bogey man did it? What's there to argue?! I did it! What's his problem?! And why didn't he ask me what I wanted? Why not ask *me* for a change, for Christ's sake?! It's my life and my problem, and no one has ever, ever asked me what I wanted! Screw 'em! Screw 'em all!"

"I hear you, Harold, and I understand why you might feel, well, manipulated, but it wasn't like that. I promise." She watched Harold's face for any sign that he was listening, let alone hearing what she needed him to try to understand. "And I still have the tapes. No one else has them, I promise. And Mr. Spencer, who only has your best interests at heart, by the way, certainly isn't going to be using anything on the tapes against you."

"Yeah, but he listened to them or can if he wants to, damn it. Now he can know that I'm a loser and that I jacked off and that girls treated me like scum, and all the other stuff about me. No wonder he doesn't come and actually spend time with me, not that I want him to. He thinks I'm a piece of shit just like everyone else. Like everyone always did!"

Harold lay down on his back with his hands over his face, as if by covering his face he could do the same with his feelings. He mumbled something about a "damn trial."

Again, Dr. Rosenthal didn't know where to begin. There was never enough time, especially, and always, it seemed, for Harold. And she sensed that he was deluding himself about what was to come.

"Harold, what did you think was going to happen to you?

You're not stupid. Didn't you realize there would be a trial and sentencing and the whole nine yards? And don't you think what has happened is a little more, well, impressive for lack of a better word, than stories about girls and teachers and your feelings of unpopularity?"

"I wasn't popular. I was never popular," Harold jumped in.

"That's not what I'm asking about, Harold. You know perfectly well what I'm asking and by avoiding the question, you are giving me your answer!" Harold was silent.

Dr. Rosenthal continued. "You've convinced yourself somehow that this is it, haven't you? That you'd somehow just stay here, walk in circles, learn to deal with the guards and grow old. Am I right? Did you trick yourself into thinking that? Did you? Because I know you're not that stupid, but you're acting as if you believe it. And you probably did it because you're scared to death of what's next. You just decided that there wouldn't be a 'next', didn't you?"

Harold spoke quietly, so quietly that Rosenthal could barely hear him. "My lawyer, Spencer, he said it was good to delay the trial, to get people to calm down or something so I'd have a better chance at a different kind of sentence. I might turn fifteen before the trial date, which is worse than being fourteen. He said he can delay, but he can't control when the judge will actually set the date. He also can't control whether the guy'll want to kill me or not."

Dr. Rosenthal turned slightly pale and lowered her head. Harold was bringing up what she had wanted to talk to him about. Enough time had passed since the shootings that first, he was going to be transferred to what was referred to as "County," an adult prison about a hundred miles northwest. This would be a much more difficult experience for him.

Even though she hoped he'd be kept apart from the main adult population until his trial, he would have to contend with some pretty rough types. All this when he already felt he was, as he described himself, a piece of shit. And yes, she was secretly terrified, and had argued with Spencer about his strategy of keeping Harold's case in a holding pattern. He had accused her of being overly sentimental and, rightfully, of being ignorant about the judicial process. But she did understand about cooling public sentiment.

At the same time, she felt it was a terrible life and death gamble with Harold's life. If he turned fifteen, the chances that he'd be tried as an adult would increase. The laws had changed in many states and one didn't have to be sixteen anymore to face the adult consequences of murder. She couldn't bear to think of what would happen to him if that were the case. She just knew he'd never make it, not in a million years. On death row awaiting execution, or for twenty-five to life, he'd either be killed or go quickly mad.

Ever since Dr. Rosenthal had realized what was going on behind the scenes, she had been having nightmares about what happens to a lost boy who kills. In this case, Harold, but regarding others as well. She was good enough at what she did to know that, contrary to public opinion, this situation was not such an aberration. Something like it, or close to it, was happening in schools all over North America.

She feared the social consequences, the missed opportunity to understand and prevent such occurrences if kids were just punished and forgotten, especially if lost children were conveniently made into adults for the sole purpose of punishment. That's the way things were, or were becoming, and how they would be for the foreseeable future. These were fearful and angry times.

"You're right," Rosenthal responded, almost forgetting what she was actually affirming. "You're . . . you're right that everything will be different if you are tried as . . . as an adult, Harold."

She saw that Harold was looking at her as if she were going to qualify or dilute the force of what she had said. "We'll cross that bridge when and if we come to it, but you're both right about what Mr. Spencer told you, and right to be afraid."

She realized that what she was about to add was as ironic as hell. *"You'd be crazy not to be."*

And, unfortunately, she knew Harold wasn't crazy. Nor were hundreds of thousands of pre-teens and teenagers just like him simmering away in dark rooms imagining how they could make themselves be of value, or just noticed, or heard in an insanely busy and indifferent world. Most of them, she knew, thought primarily about hurting themselves, not others. Increasingly inured to death and gore, cosmetic wounds, video massacres, and war games, she knew more children would die. She also knew that more would be either killed or imprisoned for committing murder on a particularly bad day.

"Have they told you when you will be transferred, Harold?"

Harold was picking at a brown mark on his blue and white striped pillow. It seemed worn from his picking at it, as if he were trying to eliminate both the stain and its mysterious source.

"Harold?"

"I *don't know*. A week, I think. I think they take me in a week. That's what one guard said."

"How do you feel about that?" Dr. Rosenthal looked away herself as she asked the question. She knew it was ridiculously clinical sounding. But she needed to ask, if only to see if he would admit his fears.

"Gee, terrific, Doc! Great! I'm hoping for a waterbed, pizza delivery and a VCR in my cell!" He clenched the fist of his left hand and punched his other hand so hard it clearly hurt all the way to his shoulder. "I'm scared to death and all, what do you think?! I'm going to die there!"

"Why're you going to die, Harold? Why there and not here?" She was hoping he didn't really know how much rougher it would be in an adult facility.

"Because . . . I *don't know*. I just know that away from here, far away, no one will know me, and it will be new and I'll be the killer kid and . . . I *don't know*."

To her amazement, it occurred to Dr. Rosenthal that he was afraid to leave what he still considered home, that this child who had killed his own parents and destroyed so many lives in his own community was afraid to leave "home," even if he *was* in prison.

"Are you going to miss being here?" she asked softly, but with a slight tone of disbelief.

"Yeah." He twirled his head in a half circle and back, and rolled his eyes up into his forehead as if he were imitating a mild seizure. "Yeah, I don't want to go."

Harold closed his eyes and shifted his head to an angle that he felt would hide his tears. Dr. Rosenthal wanted to leave her chair to sit by him, but she didn't dare move. She wasn't sure he knew she could see the tears thickening his eyelashes and spreading out at the top of his cheekbones.

"What's here, Harold?" she asked, now almost whispering so as to avoid disturbing whatever was allowing his feelings to come to the surface.

When he answered, Harold spoke so quietly that his words were barely audible. "Nothing, really. Nothing," he smirked, realizing that he didn't understand why he wanted to stay either. "It's stupid, but I might be able to do this. I mean, make it here for a while. I've never lived anywhere else — I mean in any other town — and I don't know anyone there. I know what to expect here, and the guards are going to start all over again, going at me and all, and, I don't know. I just don't want to go." He wiped away his tears abruptly, as if he just realized they had meandered down his cheeks.

"Does it mean that maybe all this becomes more real, Harold? Does it make you think more about what you did?"

"No! Maybe! I don't know. I just don't want to go to a big prison, with big dudes and fags and dope heads and have no privacy and get beat up and have a trial and . . . whatever. I don't want to do this anymore."

Rosenthal was half-fascinated and half-startled, afraid. "Do what? You don't want to do what anymore?"

"I don't know. This. Be here. Talking about this. Going there because I killed people. I don't want to be this anymore. A murderer and all."

Increasingly curious, Dr. Rosenthal pushed. "What were you before, Harold? I mean, a week ago? Even yesterday or last night? Since it happened, have you sometimes not been a . . . a . . . murderer?"

"Sometimes. Sometimes I'm just here like I'm in my room, staying away from my dad and avoiding watching my mom catch hell and all. Sometimes, a lot of the time, it's not real what they say I did. It's just kind of a cool dream, or a game or something. Then. . . ."

"Then what?"

"Then, nothing!" Harold half-shouted. "Nothing! Nothing! Nothing!" He shoved his face into the stained pillow. Dr. Rosenthal suspected he was crying again, but she decided to push anyway. She was fascinated by what she thought she was hearing.

"Do you mean 'nothing' as in there is nothing left for you? That you've killed and, well, now your life as it was is over?"

"My life sucked!" he yelled, the volume muffled by the pillow.

"Yes, but it was safe, wasn't it, Harold? It was familiar and routine and you could control much of it. Am I right?"

"I don't know, okay?! I don't know! Just leave me alone! Why don't you just leave me alone now?! I'm going to go up to County and get punched out and wear another number and play killer kid 'til they decide what to do with me! Then I'll just die. One way or another, I'll fucking die!"

Dr. Rosenthal saw a new, or at least revised, side of Harold. She realized that she had come at the right time. He was definitely affected by her presence, by the presence of another relatively sympathetic human being. And he was scared to death. Finally. Clearly, he was closer to really being aware of and thinking about what he had done. She didn't know whether it was the thought of the move or just time itself. She felt it was probably a combination of the two.

However, there were to be no more questions. Harold made it clear that he had had enough. He lay on his side, curled up, with his back to his visitor and his hands clasped around the back of his head. Dr. Rosenthal knew when someone had gone into a mental and physical shell, and he was definitely gone. She left any further questions unasked. She fell silent and tried to imagine the hell fire burning in this strange boy's mind and heart. Then she quietly left.

She spoke to the guards and recommended a suicide watch for the rest of the week. She made a mental note to try to book a space of time on the day of his transfer. He was going to need any and all familiar faces, objects or moments that he could get. After all, it would mark the beginning of nothing.

EIGHT

The Winding Road

THE BUMPING AND WEAVING of the police van made Harold sick. The wrist and ankle chains kept him from being able to see from the back of the van where there was a mere crack between himself and the guards, but no window. Adding to his apparent travel sickness and white-lipped terror was the fact that he had awakened to a nightmare.

He had had no warning. But this was the day. He had spoken to Dr. Rosenthal just two days ago and he was counting on having a week or so to get himself together so he could try not to panic when the time came for his transfer. He had even tried to send word to his sister to let her know that he would be leaving in a week or so. He couldn't have prepared for this.

They woke him at 4:30 A.M, much earlier than usual. He was given a different, gray, zip-up, one piece work suit, and shoved out of his cell before he could even go to the bathroom. For the first thirty seconds, he thought he was dreaming.

Harold noticed the new guards were being rougher than usual — for guards, that is. And the old ones were looking at him with more disdain than any of the guards had since he had first been locked up. Earlier, when he thought about leaving, he imagined that a few might want to say goodbye or something, but they all just glared at him, almost with drooling disgust.

He couldn't figure it out — the rough awakening, which he finally figured was an early transfer, and the renewed, almost rabid hostility from the guards. But as they were half-pushing and half-dragging him through the various checkpoints and down a long dark hall to a rear exit, he heard them muttering to each other in fits and starts of fresh fury.

He heard the same kind of swearing and violently spat words he had heard the day of his arrest. He strained to listen. He was so scared, he suddenly noticed he couldn't breathe, and hadn't been for the last several minutes.

"Bastard, whacko kid!" one guard swore to the other. "What the hell are they all turning into, for Christ sake?!"

"Killers, man. Killers!" replied the other guard nearest to him. "Killing means nothing to these little shits, and then they cry abuse, molestation or whatever, to get out of it! I'm sick of it. We should shoot the frigging mutants. Shoot, stab and torture them the way they done to others!"

Harold shivered, continuing to wonder why they were ranting with renewed rage. Most people just treated him with quiet disinterest at this point. One or two of the older guards were sometimes even nice to him. He wondered if there was something new, something about him that he didn't even know about in the papers or on TV or something that had set them off.

He tensed with mounting fear and strained even harder to listen. He wasn't thinking, per se. He was in pure survival mode, but he was almost sure he wouldn't make it. He'd never felt so close to or likely to be killed.

"How old was the bastard? Thirteen?" asked the smaller guard on Harold's left side.

"Yeah, named John or Jake or Josh or something, in Florida. And the kid he killed, the little girl, was eight. Same age as mine. If I got my hands on him first, I'd beat the little prick to death!"

This guard, flanking Harold's other side, was huge, like a TV wrestler, and could have accomplished his stated solution with one effortless swipe of his arm.

His colleague nodded, shook his head, and let out a tight whistling sound. "Kept her little body under his frigging bed! Do you believe it?! For four days, he hid her, slept right on her, all to do with being rejected by her older sister or something."

The big guard tightened his grip on Harold's arm and pulled harder. There would be bruises there later, fingerprints symbolic of the man's barely contained urge to personally impose a brutal justice.

"That's what I heard. Don't have a burger with me, and I'll kill your sister! Don't let me play ball with you guys, and I'll mow you down with an Uzi! Gimme your Nikes or you're dead! Bang! What the hell are we producing?! A bunch of little killers! Casual little killers! At least now they have to pay! None of this boohoo "get me a shrink" stuff! They're going to face it like you and me, buddy. Gassed, zapped or making license plates 'til they drop. The days of whining and hosing juries are oo-*ver*! Praise God!"

"You got it, man. Praise God! This shit has to stop."

Harold got it. Or he thought he did. Some other kid must have done it, killed another kid. But this sounded really weird. He knew from his own case that things could really be exaggerated at the beginning, but he still felt sick at the thought of a kid killing a little girl and then stuffing the body under his bed. He knew bodies smelled, even after a day. This kid must have been crazy, he thought. He thought of the little girl.

Then, even as he was being pushed into the dark van, with no loose limbs with which to balance himself, he thought of his sister. He couldn't stand the thought of that happening to her, especially when she was too little to understand and still thought people were good. His eyes burned with tears.

He wasn't sure why he was crying, nor was he in the mood or environment to think about it. Was it for his sister? The little girl? Was it because he was being transferred?

Could he somehow not stand the idea of being put in the same category of someone who would kill a little girl? He held his feelings in as much as he could. A few tears escaped which he couldn't even wipe away. His nose ran, causing him to sniff as he tried to keep what he couldn't hold in from dripping into his mouth.

"What's wrong with you, killer boy? Got a touch of a cold, do you?" asked the bigger, more frightening guard. "Gee, hope you don't die of pneumonia or something. We want to see you fry, m' boy!"

With that, the guards laughed, slammed the back of the van, triple locked it, and swung into the front of the truck. They continued to laugh as they accelerated into the early morning darkness.

The jolt of sudden movement sent Harold to the floor, face and head first. He lay there for some time, his face swollen and pressed into the scuffed and splintered wooden floor. There would be a damp, distinctly stained spot for almost a week where he had lay, wept and bled.

❖❖❖❖

After what felt like two days, when it had only been a few hours, Harold finally tried to straighten up. He heard the guards call out after stopping the van, and then it started moving again. They had stopped before. They stopped somewhere where they could park near a door and have a meal. They were joking again about their "killer boy" when they returned and got on with the trip.

At the next stop, Harold knew they had arrived and he

was scared. He had to be ready for when they opened the door. He tried harder than ever in his life to look calm and unaffected by their anger, his fear, and the pain in his head and body.

He knew it wouldn't do him any good to tell them he didn't blame them, especially about the little girl in Florida. He was an animal to them — an animal like the other kid or kids who'd been knocking people off like beer cans on a fence.

He felt a panic, a terror as hot as white coals shoot up from his stomach to his chest and throat. He'd never kill a little girl, he cried to himself as he became disoriented with panic. Just as the guards opened the door to the blinding light of another trek in chains, he threw up.

Harold tried to appear oblivious to the angry derision of his guards. In fact, their admonishments and mocking of him and his vomiting were just background noise related to the picture before him. He consciously thought that now he *was* dead. This was it. He wouldn't survive this.

The buildings were drab and huge, like chunks of a decrepit, medieval castle. There were uniformed guards with automatic weapons situated at various points along an encircling wall that defined the huge prison property. They were all watching him as he was dragged to a small hut and waited, hunched over, while his guards chatted with the prison guard who logged him in by writing some number on a worn clipboard.

He was then forced to turn and walk about 200 feet to the main building. He struggled and tripped, still unused to the baby steps enforced by his ankle chains. He was shaking and his breathing was shallow and quick. For a split second, he thought he might be having a heart attack, but then his thoughts switched to a hundred other fears, including those related to the scary men lined up along the fence on either side of the path.

They were yelling at him and laughing, calling him "baby" and "sweetheart" and other sexually taunting terms. He lowered his head and tried to hide his tears. His knees buckled as he tried to get past them, but he became involuntarily paralyzed with shock, terror and a feeling of suffocation.

His guards became impatient and, as if he were a rag doll, proceeded to drag him faster toward the main door. For the first time since he killed her, Harold silently called for his mother. He longed for the safe, controlled familiarity of his bedroom. He'd even settle for a lecture from his dad.

At the receiving desk, the guards who delivered him spent a long time filling out forms and joking with the attendant. As Harold waited, he noticed that all the guards had what looked like small machine guns at their sides, tucked into chest level, leather holsters. About twenty feet away, a guard leveled Harold with a stone-cold stare, unblinking in a combined smirk and sneer.

Harold tried to look down and away in order to escape both the power, and what felt like a warning, a guarantee of misery emanating from the man's eyes. He prayed there would be a problem with the paperwork and he would have to be taken back. There wasn't.

Harold was internally and externally examined again, forced to shower in cold water, and to put on a new prison uniform. He was taken to his cell, pushed in and told to shut up, use the toilet and wait for whatever and whenever they decided he could eat or drink.

Pointing to the filthy, bare cot with his eyes, the escorting guard told him to jump up and down if he got cold. The guard found this last remark hilarious and left Harold standing in the center of his new home shivering so violently, one could have sworn he was being electrically shocked.

He stood there, stunned, helpless, involuntarily jerking, and numb with terror for three hours. All he felt was a vague sense of hoping to die.

Harold had barely made it to the rusted cot, and was still confused and almost hallucinatory with terror, when he felt himself launched into the air. He had been lying on his side, facing the paint-chipped brick wall with his knees drawn up to his chin, when he was grabbed and flung like a stuffed animal. His shoulder and the right side of his head hit the adjacent wall. Only semi-conscious, he didn't look up.

"Din Dins, Harry boy," a middle-aged guard said as he placed a tray of steamy beans at Harold's side. "We want to stay fit now, don't we, you little shit?"

He turned to leave, and as he locked the metal door with a small middle window two thirds of the way up, he added, "After all, we want to be in good shape for the juice!" He meant the array of gases and chemicals used to put someone to death in the gas chamber.

Harold could hear the guard getting great enjoyment out of his remarks as the heels of his heavy, steel-toed, prison-issue boots echoed along the empty, cement hallway. Harold noticed steam rising from the tin plate and then closed his eyes again.

He was feeling more now, and was more aware, but he tried not to think — about anything. He had no place to go in his thoughts, past or present, in which to hide or to calm himself. His mind was no longer as receptive to retreat. It was too full. It was overflowing with images of hateful, spitting wet mouths, of screams, of a dead little girl, and of pain.

He willed himself to sleep. Even nightmares would be better than consciousness. And he prayed for the first time in his life. He prayed to be able to sleep, and that he would wake up and find that all of this had been a bad dream.

It was fine with him that he was left alone for three days. The guards told the warden that he had resisted and they kept him in his cell for the extended time — with very little food — as a kind of solitary confinement.

Harold just went in and out of sleep, working harder and harder at it as his shattered shoulder swelled up and caused him increasing pain. Fortunately for Harold, he had also incurred a mild concussion, so he was prone to sleep anyway — the worst and best thing one can do with a head injury, depending on one's priorities.

Then, on the fourth morning, after being awakened at 5:00 A.M., and treated to some strange tasting porridge and burnt toast, the guards came, unlocked his dark cell and chained his ankles and wrists. He didn't know why and he didn't try to figure it out. He just waited, unable even to relieve himself, for another few hours. For all he knew, this was part of his new routine. And waiting things out had become as natural as breathing.

Just before 9:00 A.M., the guards returned. They lifted and pushed Harold out of his cell and roughly urged him down the hall to the visiting room. Once he caught on that this was where he was being taken, he wondered who would come to see him.

His sister? He didn't think so. She had suddenly decided that she hated him after all, and had written that she never wanted to see his murdering face again. She had said something about her therapist helping her to see reality.

He vaguely hoped that it was Rosenthal who was there, but doubted it. She might come at some point, but not now. She wouldn't even know he'd been transferred, and he wasn't sure why he'd ever put any hope into her visiting again at all, regardless of where he was. She was neither his shrink, nor his friend. He had merely put her into some category by desperate default.

He stumbled into the glass partitioned room, trying to look less disoriented and fearful. He wished it could be his mom there. He knew she would forgive him anything.

"Harold? Over here!" a man's voice called out in a muffled,

embarrassed kind of way. He also sounded impatient and nervous. "Hurry up! Over here." It was then Harold noticed that it was his lawyer.

He made his way to cubicle number four, sat down and picked up the filthy telephone receiver as best he could with his now permanently injured arm. The mouthpiece wreaked of bad breath, cigarettes, even vomit. He was glad that he was getting good at closing down more of himself than ever, more than just his feelings. He was learning how to close down his senses too.

"How you doin'?" his lawyer asked without looking up. He appeared to be concentrating on removing papers from his shiny, leather briefcase. "Managing in your new lodgings?"

He still didn't look up. It was as if he were trying to block Harold out, as well as the surroundings. Since Harold had entered the room, the man had glanced at his watch three times.

"Okay," Harold responded, feeling even less confident than before that this guy gave a damn about him. Plus, he had expected the stupid question about how he was doing, and had the urge to tell this guy that he had never had so much fun in his life, nor been as healthy or happy.

He thought the guy must be retarded or something to ask something so idiotic — especially with Harold's arm hanging out of joint like a stuffed sock, and one side of his head looking as if he had a hairy melon attached to it. Just in case, however, Harold tried not to lose it. He didn't want to turn this guy off. He was the only help he might have, so he kept his mouth shut.

"Good. Well, we have a few things we have to get straight today and we don't have much time, so. . . ."

"Where's Rosenthal?" Harold interrupted.

"What?"

"Where's Dr. Rosenthal? She coming, or what?"

Spencer looked irritated and impatient. "I don't know, or

I don't think so. That's up to her at this point. But it would just be to visit, not to. . . ."

"Help," Harold interrupted again. "It wouldn't be to help me, or make me feel better or listen to me, right? She'd just have to come to party with me in this dump!"

"Look, kid. . . ."

"My name's Harold."

"Sorry. Harold. Let's just do our work here, okay? Regarding Rosenthal, well, I think she told you, we can't have anyone, well, actually treating you until after the trial. We don't want anything, and I mean anything, to get out that we can't control."

"Like what? What couldn't we control?"

Spencer ran his fingers through his thinning hair and sighed. "Well, whether you thought about it ahead of time, uh, whether you were angry with someone at school. That kind of thing. We've got to weave every detail of our case to our advantage. Plus, and this is primarily why I came today, we have to get the judge to re-think his position on juvenile or family court versus an adult proceeding."

"What's he thinking about? I've heard he's already decided to try me like Jeffrey Dahmer. Try 'im. Kill 'im. That's it. Over. Everyone claps up a storm, and he gets re-elected." Harold's words were slurred, but he was amazed by his ability to converse with this strange, vigilant man.

Spencer appeared to either not hear or not appreciate the Dahmer comparison. "Well, he *is* predisposed to take this to adult court," the lawyer responded, still shuffling papers and avoiding looking Harold in the eye. "The whole country is, for Christ sake! Kids can't do this anymore and go into counseling for a week or so and then go to the prom."

He finally looked up. He looked at Harold with unmistakable contempt. "The mood has changed, I can tell you that right now!"

It was eminently clear to Harold where his lawyer's sentiments fell. "So, what're you going to do, lie about my age? Tell them I'm insane? Say I was on drugs? What?"

"Were you?" Spencer looked up hopefully. He had seen the police drug report and it was clean, but if Harold said he had done some kind of dope, they might have something to work with.

"What?"

"On drugs? Were you on something? Anything?"

"No."

"Never? You never took drugs?"

"Once maybe. Some grass. I tried it in the woods behind the school about two years ago. Somehow I don't think it would still have a strong enough effect to make me massacre my parents and some kids. Do you?"

Harold's sarcasm and general attitude weren't going over well with Robert Spencer. He didn't really like taking on kid's cases and he didn't really like kids, especially violent ones, aberrations. But there was no one else at the time he was assigned. And you don't say no when a judge assigns a case to you. Otherwise, the next time you try a case before him, you start with a minus ten. He was trying to grin and bear it.

"Listen, the point is to find *something*, smart ass. And if we don't, you're tried as an adult killer and sentenced accordingly. That sound good to you?"

"Man, nothing sounds good to me, okay? You do what you have to, to look like you're, what do you call it? Oh, like you're representing me properly, and I'll just go along, okay?"

Spencer was taking notes while Harold was talking. He didn't hear him. Either that or he was learning to ignore his client's impertinence.

"Harold, your dad ever hit you? I mean really hard and repeatedly?"

Harold rolled his eyes. "No. I mean, he belted me a few times, but he didn't beat me, if that's what you mean."

"Damn," Spencer swore, clearly disappointed. "Your mother? An uncle? A teacher? Anyone?"

"Nope."

"Did anyone ever — ah . . . touch you or, you know. . . ."

"You mean, did anyone ever jack me off, or mess around with me sexually? No. Except the cops almost."

"Okay," the lawyer raised his hand as if to say he had heard enough on that question. He kept writing and was rubbing his forehead with more intensity.

"Were you ever, ah, locked in your room for days, or, ah, not fed, or. . . ," Spencer suddenly looked enthusiastic, "made to drink booze or take medication or anything like that? "

"Nope." Harold could feel Spencer's temper rising, but what was he supposed to do? Lie? He wasn't going to pull one of those Menendez trips. People knew the conceited pricks were lying anyway. It was bullshit, pure and simple.

"Then what the hell was wrong with you, for God's sake?!" Spencer surprised both of them by momentarily dropping his professional demeanor. "Why the hell did you do it?!"

Harold looked down and sideways for the first time during the awkward interview. "I don't know. I sort of do, but don't."

"What the *hell* does that mean?" Spencer asked with impatience and obvious contempt.

"It means I don't know, that's what it means. It means I couldn't stand certain things, lots of things, anymore. I couldn't stand being with my parents, being at school, being alone. I couldn't stand *anything* anymore."

"Did you hate your parents? Did they humiliate you?"

"No, and what's to humiliate? Look at me. Wouldn't you have a hard time not humiliating me if I was your kid?"

Spencer didn't have a poker face. His non-response and facial expression indicated that he might do more than humiliate a kid like this if he ended up with one. Harold had visions of himself being put down like a pet gone bad.

"Harold, you're not helping me much here. I can't get you out of an adult judicial process unless you can give me some way of showing why or how the kid in you was driven to this. Do you understand? "

Harold was silent.

"Do you even care?! Look around you, damn you! Do you think you'll just get a few broken bones and bruises in a place like this? Do you know what you're in for, kid?!"

"Yeah, I'm in for murder," Harold answered with a sigh, knowing that's not what his lawyer meant. "And I'll get life, won't I, or the death penalty?" His voice softened. "Won't I?"

Spencer half-ignored the question. "We have to find extenuating or mitigating circumstances — something that precipitated an act of irrational rage. We have to."

As an afterthought, Spencer paused for effect. "So, before our next meeting or talk, however we do it, I want you to think about it. Okay, Harold? Think of the questions I asked you and *anything* that would explain what you did." He drew Harold's eyes to his. "Harold, you got it?"

Harold got the message. "You want me to think of something, like make something up, right?" He sneered audibly.

"I didn't say that Harold. I didn't. I just said put some more thought into it. Think of anything, anything we can use, okay?" he asked as he rose to leave.

He looked as if he couldn't get away fast enough. "Okay?" he repeated, glancing back when he was halfway out the door. The lawyer had already decided that their next meeting, if there was one, would be on the telephone. The place and the kid gave him the creeps. He wondered about the story he'd heard about the little girl who almost drowned. This kid was definitely weird. He just might have done it.

Harold watched Spencer leave as the guard took his arm and forced him to rise from the cubicle chair. He only fell twice baby-stepping his way back through the enormous building to his cell.

Left alone, Harold went into what his mother used to call one of his trances. However, she'd seen nothing the likes of his current ability to stare for hours in total silence and stillness.

He was thinking, even if it was against his will. He was thinking about how amazing it was that so much can change and nothing changes at all, and at the same time, he knew he shouldn't be at all amazed, or even give it a second thought.

Still, he was in a kind of awe over how full of crap everyone was, or of how everyone was looking for crap to use to hide crap. Everything was crap or about crap. It came to him that if anything got him in here, it would be the same thing that got him on the outside. Crap. Just more of it, deeper and denser, and with a stench that curled stomach lining. He was floating in a world of crap.

NINE

Waiting Alert

THREE WEEKS PASSED and Spencer neither called nor came back. Harold had barely noticed — only on and off in the background of his thoughts. He was trying to focus on surviving in this not very brave new world. He didn't know what to do, or if he even cared to do anything at all about checking on his case. In the odd moment of concern, he just forced himself to assume that something must be happening, somewhere on his behalf.

By law, he thought, whether Spencer liked him or not, he had to at least go through the motions of defending him. He sure didn't feel like calling and sounding like a baby who couldn't handle waiting or, more precisely, waiting in prison.

However, he had an almost festering need to call *someone*. It could be virtually anyone, just so that another human being would know where he was and the kind of place he was in. For split seconds, he willed himself to think that this might help, that someone might be able to influence someone else and have him removed from this place of constant nightmares. But who?

He had almost mustered the courage to try to use one of his bi-weekly telephone privileges to call Dr. Rosenthal. Even though he didn't *really* know her, she was still the only person he knew who was an adult and didn't seem to hate him. Even the physician and influential member of the community who had been the Connally family doctor wouldn't accept his calls.

His determination to communicate beyond the prison walls was not attached to a plan, or even a specific plea. And it wasn't like him to try to call for help under any circumstances. Moreover, he knew no one could get him out.

He wondered if his sudden need to connect had something to do with having gone from feeling invisible to feeling almost dead. The sense of being virtually dead and done with was, in a strange way, more painful than feeling unseen and unheard, and certainly more terrifying.

It was a sense, a mental and emotional space he hadn't experienced before. It was as if he were caught inside a hot air balloon and was suffocating from enclosure and hot, noxious gases. And maybe, just maybe, if someone knew he was there, trapped and gasping to stay alive, they'd puncture the hot, fleshy float and set him free. Perhaps finding just one person to come to see and be with him would relieve the suffocating feeling of gasping and floating in oblivion. He feared floating to death in publicly pleasing silence.

Less than a week after his lawyer had visited, Harold had been moved out to the main block. He was put in a new cell between a great big African American guy who yelled constantly and pounded the bars, even, it seemed, in his sleep.

An old white guy kept tapping on Harold's wall from the inside back corner. It was as if this latter, long-time inmate was trying to speak to him in some strange code. That or, Harold thought, he was crazy and just liked the sound and feel of his knuckles being torn apart on chipped cement.

Unlike the artificial but separating walls in modern neighborhoods, Harold quickly came to know his neighbors. He knew them by the various sounds they made and by how they moved around in their modest living spaces. He'd put a face to them during yard time.

They'd all stand around in bunches or alone, watched steadily by armed guards in prison issue, black jackets and dark glasses. At meals, even though he learned to keep his head down and never make eye contact, he got to identify the night farter in cell 127, the knuckle cracker in cell 101, and the guy they called "Father" in cell 163. Father read the Bible all the time and could quote any part on cue. He had a religious answer for everything, including, Harold heard one day in the yard, constipation. The man had quoted a passage from Deuteronomy.

No one taught Harold how to learn the so-called prison ropes. It was automatic, by necessity, like learning to pee into a glass bottle just for the relief. You'd learn pretty quickly if you missed, especially if you had to drink it.

He was also learning to be more invisible than ever. However, it was not an easy task — not like at home. Here, inmates saw others like him when they wanted to, and there was nothing anyone could do about it. Once any number of inmates zeroed in on you, all you could do was wait, try not to show any reaction and endure how little or how much they wanted to "beef" you.

Beef meant anything from staring at you from a few centimeters from your nose, to pushing you from one inmate to another like a human sack, leaving a space so that you ended up on your face or butt. Beefing was done to humiliate, establish dominance, or punish inmates at random. In a systematic and hierarchical form, beefing also defined traditional patterns of initiation or persecution. It was permitted in full view of the screws — the guards — and was deemed normal prison behavior.

Similarly, there were more violent, secret, or seemingly

accidental acts occurring almost hourly. Harold soon learned to just step over a bloodied body during his mandatory shower. The thing was to never get involved, never appear to be listening to any conversations, whispered or otherwise, and to never give away anything that another inmate wanted from you.

Harold missed his shower as often as he could, and rarely carried anything with him — not even a book or his watch. One guy had ripped out a hunk of his hair simply because he was dissatisfied with his own recent bleach job. Harold just reacted as if he had been slightly jostled in a crowd, even though he now sported a bald welt the size and color of an apple just left of center on the top of his head.

Though he tried to look and stay cool, Harold couldn't remember the last time he had breathed normally or kept his eyes closed for more than ten minutes, even at night in a locked cell. Inmates knew how to get into anything they wanted. If they wanted to visit, they did.

Harold had had several evening surprises, one where a skinny Haitian guy, who hadn't bothered him before, came in and stuck his tongue down his throat. Again, once he realized what was happening, Harold just lay there and waited for the guy to remove his tongue. It seemed like the thing was about three feet long and was in there for an hour, but he made it through the experience without choking or throwing up. The guy would have had someone beat him up if he had openly resisted.

Harold knew that it could have been a lot worse. He'd already had his face randomly pushed into open pants and his head pressed between muscular thighs. It had become commonplace, especially in the communal shower, to be held and pushed to his knees so that bigger, older inmates could get their kicks slapping his cheeks and mouth with huge, swinging pricks. Sometimes they came on him, sometimes they didn't. He was forced to simply accept his situation, and not look too tough or too weak.

Something dramatic was always happening right from the first day he was moved from his other, somewhat more distant cell. It was as if there had been an announcement made that he was moving and entering the more boisterous area holding the general population. All the inmates had gathered at various points along hallways and steel balconies to hoot and swear and generally gross him out. As he walked slowly with his arms full of what he had had in his old cell, his knees bent and routinely buckled under the weight of his fear.

Harold was glad to have two guards with him, but he didn't trust them. If the inmates made a move on him, he'd be dead. There were only two screws and hundreds of angry, unshaven, mostly muscular, old-looking guys watching him as if he were the fixings for a violent barbecue.

Some stared blankly at him for seconds between grunted greetings, as if sizing him up from their particular point of interest. Others just let their predilection be known right off and called, "Here wimp! Here wimp!" laughing the deep, dirty laughs of men who smoke and drink too much coffee, but move too little.

A whole row of men mooned him, exposing and wiggling their yellowed, hairy asses while making whooping sounds like excited old women. The guards just laughed and told the inmates to pull up their pants. About a half dozen managed to grab his chest or thigh as he rounded the upper corner to his new, older cell. He couldn't wait to be locked in, in spite of its yellow-brown walls and cracked, blood and barf-stained floor.

Once he was in, Harold just lay frozen on his cot, still clutching the pillow and blanket from his previous quarters. The catcalls, sexual invitations and warnings continued long after the guards had left. A guy from about five cells down kept yelling for over an hour after the others had lost temporary interest. He kept asking, "Hey, Bambi, you want to get stuck? You want to? Huh?"

When Harold didn't answer, the inmate started yelling, "Bambi's been stuck! Stuck Bambi! Bambi needs to be stuck! I'm going to have you, Bambi. You're mine, sweetie pie! You're mine!"

Harold tried to go to the place in his mind where he was deaf and usually without feelings, but it was almost impossible. He put his hands over his ears and rocked back and forth trying, somehow, to thicken the outer layer of his inner world and strengthen his inner sanctuary. He needed to block influences and actions beyond his own cell.

When he did take a closer look at his new dwelling, he noticed a stale stickiness on the floor that he didn't remember seeing when he came in. He had remained in stone cold alert mode for at least three hours, paralyzed on his virtually featherless mattress. He realized that he had both — diminished awareness of and attunement to himself and his body as he fought for inner silence.

He had urinated in his pants and on the cot and floor. It seemed long ago now since the guards had escorted him in. Hours, days, minutes? It didn't matter. Time had already changed for him. There was no time, but rather demarcations signaled by whistles, yells, and the turning on and off of lights. There was no telling how long his pants had been wet and his bare foot slumped carelessly in a puddle of cold urine.

Stunned and responding with rote obedience, it was over a week before Harold dared to make several unsuccessful requests to use the one pay telephone provided to 200 inmates. He wanted to call someone, anyone, even his lawyer if he really had one, to try to get out of there before he couldn't take it anymore or something happened. He knew something would.

It didn't take a genius to sense disaster in a place like this. In fact, it was better if you were really stupid and tried to ignore subtle and not-so-subtle signals and gut feelings. Harold knew he was going to get it — something so terrifying that he wouldn't let his imagination go all the way to visualize it. He had to call *someone.*

Again, Harold couldn't let himself see that it was an illusion, observed and left over from another life, that made him think that there was someone who would come for him. There was no one left to be outraged by where he was or worried about what might happen to him. In fact, it was a new illusion, born of complete helplessness and terror.

He tried to steady himself, his entire body cringing with vigilance, as he held on to the absurd notion that someone would come to take him home or, at the very least, to a safer, more endurable place of imprisonment. He worked at building and maintaining the belief attached to his need. He could not afford to see it as a wish or fantasy. Yet, in fact, he knew. This was precisely where everyone would have him be before being legally put to death, killed, or just dying of dark morbidity.

Harold ended up assigned to the kitchen. A guy named Deke showed him what he had to do in the way of sterilizing huge bowls the size of barrels, scraping food and other debris from wide grooves and cracks in the floor, and opening tins of anything from corn to baked beans, two hundred at a time with a hand-twist can opener. He also had to wash dishes, count reused plastic plates and cutlery, and sometimes, if he was needed, serve inmates from behind a four foot wide, metal counter.

There were other chores too, and Harold concentrated on them all as hard as he could so that he wouldn't screw up. It wasn't easy. He still shook constantly whenever he left his cell, and neither his legs nor other parts of his body would cooperate when he did.

Not long into his stay in his new quarters, Harold developed a new manifestation of fear. Little squeaky noises kept emitting from his throat, up into his jaws and out his nose. Like a twitch with sound, he was helpless to stop it and the more he tried, the more the strange, high-pitched sound betrayed his awkward terror. The involuntary nervous reactions stayed the same, with very little fluctuation, as he was poked, tripped, pushed and regularly whacked on the head during his duties and days.

Harold hid and hoarded the one mental handle he had on the outside world. He became obsessed with calling Dr. Rosenthal. There was no one else. She was the only one who *might* care and he wasn't even sure of that. Nevertheless, she was an adult, had power outside the prison walls, and could perhaps help him in some way. After all, she had spoken to him and he had told her stuff.

She would know that he didn't belong here, not in a place like *this*. Seeing her, somehow, was the only thing he could think of as a way out and, at the same time, a way to explain, complain, or just show what was happening to him. He was scrawnier than ever and weak, too weak to protect himself. He was the youngest, smallest guy in the place.

I shouldn't be here, he told himself when he was sufficiently spent to bypass rationality and accept the delusion. He hoped Rosenthal would agree and fight to get him transferred, even though she didn't owe him anything. He wished he had been nicer to her, been a gentleman the way his mother had tried to teach him to be. He wished he hadn't been so stupid, that he'd been smart enough to suck up and try to get Rosenthal to really like him, even though he couldn't remember anyone important ever feeling good about him.

In the moments when he could, he gripped the idea of Dr. Rosenthal coming for him, pounding his head on both sides with his fists if he started to feel any doubt. Luckily, he didn't talk to anyone or he might have shared and lost his illusory link, his pathetic fantasy that he could be saved. Then he'd have nothing — not even the ability to fake hope.

When his fantasy thinned or weakened with fatigue, Harold thought of his death. He was sure that he would be murdered here. Maybe soon. He hadn't even known that he cared so much about living, or cared so much about not dying, or being killed, screwed half-dead by one of the big guys who would call him sweetheart and then strangle him amid a primitive, violent moment of climax.

He also knew that he could be fatally poked any time, stabbed with one of hundreds of sharp objects hidden in pillow linings and taped atop lightbulbs. He could get it at any moment, for any reason, and for no reason at all. He tried harder to both accommodate and remain innocuous. It was a tenuous mandate for survival.

When Harold lost touch with his manufactured hope, he fell into a state of mindless torpor. Nevertheless, he usually tried to keep something in him going. He tried to find something inside that was capable of making contact, calling out, and connecting with an outside world which, even if only in the context of a legal process, shouldn't and couldn't be finished with him. He had to try to keep sneaking in living moments when he'd be able to think. He felt he had to or he'd be forgotten. It would be what they all would have wanted — not just recently, but for as long as he could remember.

He tried almost every morning to get permission to get in line to use the telephone, but if he got permission, he knew he would have to defer to virtually any inmate who pushed ahead of him. Eventually, he got curt permission from a guard who had his mind on something else. The guard didn't even know what he was answering. He just wanted Harold out of his face.

Harold knew that he had to make his call and get to the kitchen on time or he'd be in deep trouble. Most likely, he wouldn't get another chance that day, or even that week. He stood in line and minded his own business, again trying to appear as if he were prepared to stand his ground. He hadn't done this before — shifted his head back on his neck, spread his legs slightly, crossed his arms across his chest and looked at the back of another inmate's head with a pseudo-confident "don't screw with me" glare.

He was scared to death, but he knew by now that showing fear was worse than showing anger or attitude. The latter two could be useful if employed strategically. Fear made a guy raw meat. He had been finely ground hamburger since day one.

He was two inmates away from the pay phone when an inmate, four back in line, pushed three others aside, reached Harold and picked him up by one arm and threw him to the floor. He then took the same stance Harold had adopted, but it was perilously real. His huge muscles, tattoos and generously scarred face lent even more credibility to his posture.

Harold got up slowly while the line-up of hardened, sweaty men laughed at his pathetically disabled form. He had hit his head and was still seeing stars as he strained to get back on his feet as quickly as possible. Just as he had almost steadied himself, he heard his name called. He was due in the kitchen. He obeyed, swaying toward the kitchen storeroom, holding back tears of rage and frustration. He was as helpless as the chunks of meat he would slice and mash into patties to prepare for deep frying. He surreptitiously spat in every second one.

The next day, he tried a dramatic new strategy. He beckoned a screw to his cell early, his cot firmly made and his cell spotless, and practically begged the guard to let him telephone what he called *his* psychiatrist. He didn't know whether the neatness would work for him or against him, but he erred on the side of winning favor.

He didn't want anyone to have any reason to think or say he was a problem. For the same reason, he learned early, he never let on if or when he had been pushed or grabbed or hit, let alone something worse. Among other more violent consequences, the guards would perceive him as a kid who just makes their jobs more difficult.

Of course, it went without saying that he didn't snitch.

"Snitch and be snatch," he had been told, and learned early. Tell on someone, *any*one, even a screw, for *any*thing, and you were deemed weak, pathetic and a liar. You became the victim of the month for every random punch out, every sexual attack, and uncountable nights without sleep trying to stay awake to protect yourself. You also became "bitch" material – that is, you became "wife" material because you were deemed "girl-weak" and in need of protection.

Harold already knew he was on several inmates' dating lists. He didn't want to give them any incentive to send flowers. Further, he didn't want to make any of the current wives mad by appearing to be fresh competition. If anyone in this place could be called "nice," it was the wives. Stay on good terms with them, and sometimes their husbands would help you out.

So far, except at the beginning, he hadn't screwed up or done anything to provoke violent sexual punishment. Whether an inmate tried or not was another matter. Most important, he hadn't done anything to ask for it. This was small comfort in an environment with few choices and an endless array of unwritten rules and creatively cruel consequences.

When the guard arrived, looking irritated and bored, Harold started to shake unnaturally, much more dramatically than he had been from day one. He had learned a trick as a child whereby he would roll his eyes back in his head so only the whites would show. By adding body jerks, a protruding and then completely receding tongue, and thick, hanging drool, he could convince almost anyone he was having an epileptic seizure and was about to die.

It had worked wonders with new teachers. He also used to do it behind his father's back when only his mother could see. When he was much younger, his mom had to suppress laughter and sometimes couldn't and had to make up a story to explain her sudden giggle during one of her husband's lectures. It seemed like just a few years later when that, among other things, didn't make her laugh anymore.

The guard did a slow motion jolt out of his requisite lethargy. "You okay?" He moved quickly to unlock Harold's cell. "Hey kid, you okay?"

Harold made choking and heaving noises and looked up at the guard imploringly, as if he were trying to talk, but might die due to the effort and pain it caused.

"I-I n-n-need to s-see my psy-psychia . . . trist. N-need m-my me-medication," Harold stammered, clutching his throat and rolling back on his cot.

The guard forgot himself for a moment while he stared at Harold's eyes. He'd never seen anything like it. Two hard-boiled eggs — just about the ugliest thing he'd ever seen that wasn't bloody or the result of a violent injury – stuck in Harold's eye sockets.

Harold appeared to struggle to communicate that he was going crazy, was sick, and had missed an appointment with his doctor. He mumbled that he was supposed to get more medication, just before he collapsed headfirst into the hard mattress. He breathed heavily, in gasps and raspy fits and starts. The guard was more than was impressed.

Then Harold actually fell sideways and accidentally hit his head on the side of the cot because he could only hold his eyes that way for so long, and this guy was making a study out of them. For a minute there, Harold thought the screw was going to call a meeting of all the others so they could get a look. He just hoped that the idiot would do something, anything, to get him closer to a telephone and to making a call.

He was lucky. The guard didn't want any problems. He was a civil servant close to retirement. He re-locked Harold's cell and radioed the assistant warden that he'd be calling from the floor phone. Apparently, the A.W., as he was called, felt the same way about Harold's strange condition and strained request.

This was a touchy inmate and a touchy case. He could

just imagine the hell he'd get from the governor if he screwed up by not getting the kid medical care. No one had told him he had a shrink or was supposed to be on medication. He ordered another senior guard to get the full name of the boy's shrink and said he would call the doctor himself. Meanwhile, to cover himself from the get go, he had Harold brought to the clinic for an examination by the prison nurse.

Harold virtually prayed that Rosenthal would go with him on this. They both knew she wasn't his official shrink and she had been pretty antsy about talking to him the last time. He was desperate. He knew she could go one way, or no way at all, either respond in some helpful way, or shut him out completely. He didn't doubt that she'd understand that he was trying to tell her that something was wrong, that he needed to see her. He just couldn't bank on whether or not she would or could act on his strategic request.

Harold was examined, heavily sedated, and returned to his cell. With the little mental clarity left him, he waited and hoped. Several times, he thought he heard her voice and thought she was standing at the end of his bed. The bed he envisioned himself in, however, was his own in his old home, and she was whispering so as not to awaken his parents down the hall. He felt a kind of elation both because she had come and because, in his dream, his parents were resting peacefully just yards away.

By the end of the day, the medication was wearing off and Harold was fighting both nausea and a new level of desolation. Just when he thought he'd have to go to Plan B and figure out how to kill himself, a senior guard he'd never seen before brought him a note.

Anxiously, he focused and re-focused on the scrawled message, but he couldn't decipher it at first. It said something cryptic, as if Rosenthal had known he'd get the message second hand. She would be in touch and would contact him as soon as possible.

He hoped this meant she would come, but, just in case it would help, he worked at focusing on her coming. He had always had a tendency to over-analyze, make negative predictions, and to temper his expectations. He forced himself to imagine and anticipate a visit.

TEN

Dread Talking

D R. ROSENTHAL'S SUPPLY OF CASSETTES and another handheld tape recorder arrived two days later. She had included a note, written to both comfort Harold and to instruct him to start speaking again, to send her two full tapes at a time and she would respond as best she could. She also reminded him that his case was pending and that she had to work at getting a new level of permission to see him.

Unbeknownst to Harold, Sandra Rosenthal was furious. Even though she was neither able nor inclined to take Harold on full-time as a patient, she was appalled that the system offered him no support during this phase of the judicial process. She had little doubt that he badly needed help.

Yet, without having been tried, and theoretically "innocent until proven guilty," he was in an adult prison with no protection. Not only was he being left to his own resources in a death trap, he was being denied what she considered basic medical help during a post-traumatic period.

Rosenthal couldn't believe how the system was turning on and at youth. "No more Mr. Nice Guy" from the courts.

The public had had it, and they were voting and otherwise supporting tough sentences and rough treatment of youthful offenders, especially killers. The demand for "no tolerance" was clear and intensely articulate, driven by deep-seated fears. There was little *she* could do for Harold other than provide him with someone to talk to.

Harold would have preferred a visit, but he must have played with the recorder and flipped the cassettes around for at least an hour, as if they were rare components of a coveted game. He savored the fact that he could talk into them again whenever he felt like it.

He felt as if he had something special and secret that the other inmates didn't have. And he had been pleased to note that each cassette displayed a little *PRIVATE* sticker. He didn't have anything that was private anymore and those labels gave him a sense of importance. Yet, he knew he had to be careful with the tapes once he was ready to relay them.

He knew that if the guards were in the mood, they would listen to them. He also knew that if they were in another mood, a worse one, the cassettes would never make it out of the prison. He'd have to worry about that later. First, he wanted to put himself on tape. This was his conduit to someone outside who would listen. He'd work out the logistics of getting the tapes beyond the walls when he had finished his first two.

In a whisper, with his head between a thin pillow and the mattress, he started to speak, but he had to start and stop about ten times. He had almost forgotten who he was, how he spoke, and what he wanted to say.

❦❦❦❦

It's bad, Rosenthal, real bad. You're, well, like, a lady and all, so I won't tell you everything or, well, you'd find it kind of gross, if you know what I mean. But if I slip, and forget or something and tell you stuff that's not too nice, I'm sorry, 'kay? If I really get going, I might not be able to control what I say.

And it's cool to have someone to talk to finally and I'm excited and might let loose.

I have to listen real careful while I do this because I'll get really beat up bad tomorrow if some guy hears me talking to my bed like a sucky girl.

Also, the guards come by real quiet. You don't even know they're there until they shine their lights in your face, so I have to watch for that too. You have to watch for lots of things in here.

Actually, I have to watch for everything. You don't even take a piss without working it all out ahead of time. It's kind of like a life strategy, one that even includes when you sigh or take a deep breath, when and if you scratch your ass, and when and where you piss.

Making a phone call is like trying to climb Everest in bare feet, I swear. My dad used to talk about politics and stuff at the offices he went to, but he doesn't know politics from nothing! If he tried his pseudo-smart, nice-guy, let's-just-work-this-out-together approach in here, he'd get a filed down piece of pipe in his gut.

You learn fast, I'm telling you. *Real* fast. I'm still just keeping out of everyone's way.

I work in the kitchen and have gotten pretty good at cleaning, even serving, but like I said, you have to remember not to forget where you are. Day before yesterday, a guy wanted more fake potatoes, but I couldn't go against the orders from the cook and the guards who say one serving only. He told me, "Never mind the orders — give me what I want!"

I spooned him some, and he wanted more, so I spooned again. I couldn't believe it, but he grabbed me by my neck anyway, hauled me clear across the counter onto the floor, dumped his plate on me and smeared the potatoes into my face. He added a gallon of ketchup and rubbed it all in some more so I looked like I had pus and blood coming out of my mouth and nose, even my ears.

I think he broke my nose and it seemed an awful long time before about five guards came and pulled him off. All the guys were cheering him and telling him to, well, to, "Cream the wimp!"

If I'm not careful, I'll be a girl here, if you know what I mean. Especially if I cry, tell on someone, or smile at anyone. No chance of that, for sure! So, when the guards who knew what happened asked what happened, I said I fell over the counter and dropped plates on my head. Sort of hard to do, but that's not the point. You have to pass the tests — all of them — with the other guys and the guards.

Come to think of it, I have. I don't think you need to hear about *that*, but let's just say, day two in the washroom, when I couldn't hold it anymore, I didn't make it to the can because this guy blocked my way. So, I did it right in front of him, which is what he wanted. Then he made me look at it and touch it. It was sort of like chunky dog food, but smelled worse.

It wasn't so bad after I could finally get away and puke. My own shit wasn't much worse than other shit in here, if I can make a joke. I'll try to make as many jokes as possible, okay? I think I'm going to need to while I tell you this stuff.

I've kind of been wondering where everyone is. Or where *anyone* is. The lawyer guy, Spencer, came, but he didn't seem to like me too much. So, what else is new, huh?

He kept asking me things that didn't have anything to do with my being here, getting out, or getting a fast trial. To be honest, I hadn't even thought of a trial. I still don't, but I still think I need to get out of here. I mean, what was wrong with where I was? I remember what you told me about not going to juvenile, but I didn't think that was written in stone.

How long will I be here, and is something being done or said about me out there? I feel like they just put me here and that's it. I feel sick. It makes me feel real sick when I think that way, but sometimes I can't help it because I get no phone calls or visitors and all the other guys here just take it like it's their home.

Some guys, a lot of guys, even like it here — wouldn't want to be out or anything. They're the guys you try not to bother or, I guess if you're staying a long time, you make them your friends. They control everything. They get cigarettes, chocolate bars, cool sweatsuits, and conjugal visits. You know, they get to have an hour of sex in a trailer once a month with someone who says she's a wife, a real girl. They also get dope, lots of it, and sometimes sell it or use it to buy loyalty. They're like the owners of the place and everyone else is like sort of renting from them and answering to them in other ways.

You don't even go in the shower when they're there unless they say it's okay. And if you don't shower, the guards yell at you and you lose privileges, like pissing when you need to and eating, or getting a book from the useless library. So, you kind of have to do as you're told, but not be a wimp at the same time. It's sort of hard. But I'm trying to hold on and all, until . . . well, until some adult from out there tells me what's going to happen to me. It just scared the hell out of me to say that. Do *you* know what's going to happen to me? Is anybody deciding? How come no one tells me anything? How come it's like I'm already here and everything is settled, but I'm still waiting? Maybe it's some kind of trick. I have to stop talking now.

Last night, it took me all night to clean myself and my bed. You have to clean real quietly so no one hears, but all you have is a toilet to get water out of. I tell you, I never did what my mom called laundry before I came here. If she could see me now! It stinks in here and so do I, but my overalls look clean and they'll only be wet for another day or so.

I have to talk to you. I figured that out a few days ago, or yesterday, or maybe this morning. It's hard to tell days here because the light's always the same, unless you get to go out to the yard. The guards could play with the lights and have us all think day was night and night was day. It's like I'm dead or something if no one from out there knows what's happening to me in here, or if no one cares or can smell my shit or see my mashed, crooked nose, or tell me what day it is. It's weird, but I feel like that, you know? Like, if no one sees what happens to you, or you can't tell anyone, then you're dead and gone. At first, I didn't think I'd tell you stuff like that, but what should I tell you about? The weather? There's no weather here. Just barometric pressure.

Do you know how my sister is? Hold on. I have to st . . . stop or . . . just wait a minute and I'll be back. Don't fast forward, 'kay? Just going to take a break. You can too, but please don't go out or anything, okay? Just wait a minute, and listen some more? Wait. Okay?

❖❖❖❖

You there? Of course you are if you can hear my voice. You can pick and choose when to listen to me, but sometimes I feel like asking you to listen to the whole thing through without stopping to listen at another time. I try not to think of you stopping the tape, sort of putting me away to do something else. I also hate to think that you might rewind and play some parts of what I say over again. I hate it. I mean, I can't be careful enough in what I say to make sure it could be listened to twice and not sound more stupid the second time. It's sort of like giving my dad an explanation for something I did on tape. I mean, you're not like my dad, but I still don't want something I get up the courage to say once, listened to twice. Do you know what I mean? It's okay if you don't.

Of course, I haven't seen Jessica since that really weird first visit. She could come if she wanted to, but I don't mind if she doesn't. I didn't want her to come here in the first place, and I wouldn't want to have to look in her beautiful face again. Imagine what I've done to it.... She has incredible eyes, but they were dull and almost black when I saw her, and I just know they've gotten worse. I understand these things. Once, when her boyfriend dumped her for someone he met at college, her eyes went dark for months and she barely spoke. I bet they look like empty holes in a skull now, and that somewhere inside and past them, she dreams that my parents still exist. I can't stand that she has stopped her life and not gone back to school. I heard that she was living with friends before I came here, but I wish she'd go back and score big time at university and make sure she isn't, like, destroyed by everything. I don't want to destroy my sister.

Between you and me, I didn't even want to destroy my. . . my parents, or even those kids. I was just sick of being invisible and having no one care to know what I thought and who I was. I mean, not something special or anything, but just something, a real person like everyone else.

Funny, now everyone *thinks* they know me, but they don't. I don't know which is better. Not to be known and to be alone, or to be known, but not known, and be squished in a dirty old building where everyone knows the smell of your shit. I know which one I'd choose now, but I don't think of that in here much. I can't. I push it away so fast it's like I never thought it.

Can you possibly find or phone Spencer and ask what's going on? I mean, you don't owe me any favors or anything, but I need to know something, to have something to hold onto in here. I need to know why it's taking so long to go to court and all.

I heard something about changing where I'd be tried because everyone would just vote to fry me in our county, but why does that take so long? I'm hoping if I don't lie and I tell the jury and the judge the truth, they will see that this is overkill. Bad word to use, I guess.

Can't they see that I'm not really a maniac? I couldn't take anymore. I went into a kind of trance and couldn't stand to have feelings. It always hurt too much. Too much at school, too much at home, too much when I thought someone liked me, and too much when what I always knew would happen, happened — when people I thought liked me suddenly didn't. In fact, all of a sudden, they'd hate me or be afraid of me. I'd have to swallow so hard sometimes to keep from crying, it'd hurt my entire body.

I know I should've killed myself instead of doing what I did, and I can't explain why I didn't, but if someone powerful understood maybe I could be somewhere else. Funny thing is, if my dad were alive, he'd be making a big stink just to get attention and to get his picture in the paper. I mean, he'd want to get me out of here too, but part of that would be to look like a cool, intelligent father.

So, can you phone Spencer? Or somebody? Is there anybody else working on this? Most of the time, I don't even picture Spencer working on it. It was pretty clear he hated me. He didn't dare look at me as if what I did is catching and he might kill his kids or something.

It's like I do something like this, which is pretty damn bad, I admit, and then I'm suddenly not a human being anymore. It's like I'm dead too. Maybe they're all hoping I'll die here. It'd be reported in the newspapers and on TV and the story would be over. Mine, at least.

I don't mean to try to be deep or anything, but I think if I were an older guy, like my dad's age or something, and I blew someone away at a gas station, I'd have a better lawyer. At least someone would know where I was and meet with me and stuff. Probably would've been to court by now too and my lawyer would've made a deal on a technicality or something and I'd know where I stood.

I think I'm far away because all of you need me to be hidden away with the really big, bad guys who'll probably kill me because I'm too much for you guys, for anyone out there to handle or to think about. And it's the same damn story. I was too much to deal with *before* I went kind of mental and no one wanted to get near me then either. Now I'm out of sight and out of mind. Even the parents of the kids I shot can rest easier. Don't think I don't know that they'll rest even easier if they find out I'm dead. Better still, mutilated, dead.

Anyway, phone Spencer if you can. Suddenly, I don't really give a damn. He's probably doing nothing for nothing. I mean for me — nothing for me. Something for something, nothing for nothing. That's what my dad always used to say, along with garbage in, garbage out, like he had made it up himself or something.

My teachers and Tarkin used the expression too. I wonder why they liked it so much, even though it's obvious what it means. Of course if you take in shit, you'll give out shit, but they'd use it for everything, like TV, books, movies, swear words and on and on. They should've applied it to their own way of treating some kids. Just like my dad who only got happy when I did something to please him that wasn't really me. That was supposed to be good stuff in. Supposedly, good stuff was supposed to come out. I'm not sure from where, but it was supposed to suddenly come out and I'd be a good guy and less of a failure. I guess, no, I *know* not enough good stuff ever came out of me — just garbage. Garbage, garbage, garbage, and then the shit hit the fan!

I'm going now, okay? So, goodbye. Talk back? Soon? It'd sort of be like being real and still living with someone.

◅▻◅▻◅▻◅▻

Dr. Rosenthal didn't receive anything until a week after Harold had filled two tapes and immediately registered them for delivery. She cringed when she did get a chance to listen, and was dismayed, but not surprised, that Harold had placed an unrealistic amount of hope in her, particularly in her ability to affect the system in some way. If anything, meddling would just make things worse.

She was also amazed and saddened by Harold's intuition about being hidden away, forgotten, because she knew that was exactly what the community wanted and was, in fact, doing. There had been talk of not only trying him as an adult, but of considering the death penalty. Were this to have happened in another state, Harold *would* be facing death. She knew he knew, or he suspected, that he was being socially and legally shunned, but she wondered if it would be beneficial to tell him, to confirm his instincts. He was remarkably savvy for a young teen, even for a teen killer.

Yet, there were contradictions. On the one hand, he suspected that he was being forgotten and, on the other, he seemed to think something could be done to lighten things up for him. But there was no way. He had become a symbol of the unpredictability and omnipresence of a growing evil. Few saw him as a disturbed child who merely acted out by mass murdering. She couldn't say that she blamed them really. But she also knew that the manic sensationalism of tabloid journalism hadn't helped. And it seemed that that kind of sadistic, cannibalistic pseudo-reportage had come to dominate much of modern journalism.

She also knew that his lawyer had all the latitude he wanted in delaying or preparing either a decent or inadequate defense for Harold. No speedy trial principle was being uttered in the county halls in relation to *this* case. In fact, she knew for a fact that Spencer and his family had been receiving hate mail. He had tried to excuse himself from the case, but the circuit judge wouldn't hear of it.

He resorted to letting it be known, if cautiously, because he could be brought before a bar review board, that he didn't *want* to represent the killer kid — especially the one who'd killed children at the same school where he dropped off his two little girls each day. The best he felt he could do was go for a weak plea. In his mind, he couldn't see himself taking this mess to trial and associating himself with any degree of passion or, for that matter, even rote duty, with Harold. In fact, he wouldn't.

Only when the judge or the prosecutor pushed him to get on with it would Spencer shift from doing the bare minimum. He had done all the law required to show that the client was, in theory, being represented. He dreaded doing more. He knew he didn't have the stomach for it. What was worse, for a defense advocate, he wished the kid were dead. It kept him awake, but not because he felt guilty about wanting the kid to die. He just couldn't stand being so clearly and publicly on the wrong team in a game that he felt was justifiably fixed.

ELEVEN

Sister Fact

Hᴀʀᴏʟᴅ ʜᴀᴅ ᴊᴜsᴛ ʀᴇᴄᴇɪᴠᴇᴅ another letter from Dr. Rosenthal when he was told to leave his almost completed kitchen duties and return to his cell. There was another piece of official mail for him and prison regulations established that anything resembling a document must be delivered to the inmate in his cell. This way, the chances of it being lost, taken, or torn up in a fight were considerably reduced.

The envelope had been hand-delivered, marked "Important," and had a doctor's return address at the top left corner. The official nature of the correspondence increased the importance of its being handled properly. Any legal or medical correspondence was to be delivered to an inmate immediately.

Harold waited, wondering why he had been called to his cell, and then was startled when the guard hit the side of his cell with a nightstick and shoved the envelope between the bars.

"What's this?" Harold asked without thinking. As soon as he opened his mouth, he wished he hadn't.

"How the hell do I know, you little whack off?!" The guard

turned sideways and half-turned back. "I'll bet my dick it's not love letters from somebody's heart!" The guard cracked up at his own one-liner. Harold could hear his laughter, then the fading echo of his cackle as he ambled back to his station.

Harold put Dr. Rosenthal's letter aside, already having a sense, but fearful, of what this latest document would say. He picked up the handsome gray envelope with a new doctor's name and address on it. He looked at the credentials; it was another shrink.

Why would a shrink I've never heard of be writing me? he wondered. He tried to open it without tearing what was inside. *Weird*, he thought as soon as he saw the handwriting.

It was his sister's – probably, he discerned, because a shrink she was seeing forced her to write it, but he didn't want to read it. Yet, he longed to. He couldn't bear to read what she felt, but he couldn't stand not knowing. The thick bond paper shook in his hands as he focused and stared at his sister's carefully, if shakily, woven penmanship.

Dear Harold,

I haven't written you yet since speaking because I haven't known what to say to you. I'm sure you can imagine that there are few words to neatly apply to either of our current states, let alone that of Mom and Dad.

I guess I should tell you, and my psychiatrist agrees, that I am very angry with you. I don't feel it really, though. At least, not often. Most of the time, I feel nothing, as if the ground has caved in beneath me, and my life and heart have been ripped from me without warning. You didn't kill me, but you did in a way. The girl I was will never be again, and my sense of the world, and of life, are forever altered. Needless to say, my sense of my little brother has also "changed" — such a tidy word for lost, gone, blasted away, even dead. I feel as if you, and we, died too. That you killed us all, along with those dear children. I wish I understood why. I wish I could make sense of the nightmare that our lives have become. I wish I could wake up.

I do often wonder how you are doing there. I have heard that it is a terrible place and that young teens have not been put there in the past. I wonder what has been done to you, whether anyone is friendly toward you, how you are surviving. You were always such a loner. I can't imagine how you live in such noisy, crowded and rough conditions. The Harold I knew, the "far off" Harold, couldn't have. Generally, people are treating me nicely, with a strange and sometimes strained kind of sympathy. Others either won't talk to me, or say things to me that make me cringe with fear and disgust. I understand why, but there are days when it is so hard to be the sister of the killer. So hard, in fact, that I even left school because I was no longer me there, but the sister of the schoolyard mass murderer. Funny, what bothered me most was the fact that no one ever mentioned Mom and Dad. No one seemed to care that they died too, and that they, too, had a life they deserved and wanted to live.

I am seeing a psychiatrist, but I can't say it is helping much. I am on two medications that just make my mouth dry and movement difficult. They don't take away the nightmares, the longing, or the trying to understand. I still wake up wanting to go to the house and talk with Mom or ask Dad's advice.

I had a proper funeral for them two weeks after they died. The Andersons helped with the arrangements. They even held the get-together at their house after the funeral. Mom and Dad are buried out in Grafton, in a lovely cemetery called "Singing Meadows." They are side-by-

*side with one tombstone representing their lives. The
engraved script says, "Two people, partners loved." I
thought I would keep it simple, especially for the gawkers.
People, strangers, drive by and walk around the
gravestones everyday looking for the graves of the
murdered parents. The children's graves, by the way, are
in the town cemetery and are left alone. Interesting, I
think. Mom and Dad were rarely mentioned on TV and
in the papers, but after, later, they were what people
wanted to see. I started seeing my therapist after I went
out there one day and attacked the strangers like a mad
woman. I screamed that they were sick and perverse and
insensitive, and I chased one family all the way to their
car. They called the police and the sheriff was pretty good
about it — just sent me to the hospital and had me
sedated. But then, and now, there is never enough
"sedation." I miss them so much, I can't imagine living.*

*I even miss you. You as you, not as what happened to
you to make you do this to us. Often, I wish I had been
home. If I couldn't have stopped you, I would be with
them. Dead, unable to hear or see the gawkers, instead of
alive, but unable to breathe, let alone eat, or sleep or read
or even go for a walk. I might come to see you one more
time. My therapist says I should "confront" you. He says
that I still love you and that I need to be sad with you, as
opposed to alone and angry. Sometimes I wonder if he
understands at all. This certainly isn't your garden-
variety life issue. I have no one left but you – Harold the
murderer who killed my mom and dad. What does one do
with that? And who am I to become? You are defined,
and your future will be decided (I hear your lawyer is
cutting a deal), but it isn't so easy for me. I apparently
have choices, but I can't see or fathom any. And I have
no strength for living, let alone choosing.*

I hope you're doing okay under the circumstances. And
I hope it will be alright if I decide I can come to see you
again. I'm not sure I can, so don't get all upset.
Anyway, it will be different and worse than last time
when it hadn't really hit me yet. It would probably be like
two total strangers meeting. We aren't as we were.
Nothing is the way it was. It and we will never be again.
I know I warned you during our short phone
conversation when I lost control and said some dreadful,
but honest, things to you. I shouldn't have called you a
murderer, but I don't know how else to put it. You killed
our parents. Enough for now.

Your Sister,
Jessica

The pages fell from Harold's hands the way a magazine
would were someone to fall asleep while reading. He shook
from head to toe, dragged from rationality by feelings so strong
that they felt more like electrocution than sentiments. His
scalp and his face tingled and then stung with the sense of a
million pins being stuck into his skull by an invisible torturer.
As the pain became worse, he scratched his head with his
untrimmed nails, and then his face, eyes and neck.

He was unimpressed with the fact that his hands were
red, dripping with blood, and he had no mirror in which to
see the slashed image of his face and head. They were roseate,
swelling, as blood oozed steadily from deep, jagged grooves
that zigzagged across his cheekbones and jaw. One ear appeared
slightly torn at the base, and his eye sockets were circled pools
of blinding blood. He had no awareness, let alone concern
with the fact that he was blind in moist darkness.

Harold didn't show for supper and after several calls on
the P.A. system, a guard marched angrily to his cell to declare
the punishment for missing duties, as well as the meal call. No
one had been concerned that he had might have to escape,

just that he was cheeky and stupid enough to break the rules.

When the guard found him, he lay naked, his head and shoulders in a pool of some dried and some moist blood. The guard immediately concluded that he had been the victim of an inmate vendetta or had made a strange kind of suicide attempt. He put in a U-3, an emergency call of the highest order, and a half dozen guards came running.

When Harold awoke in the infirmary, he was virtually swaddled. His head, neck and hands were wrapped with gauze, and he could feel a dull pressure in several spots on his face. He had had stitches and was still under a local anaesthetic. A male nurse came in just after he came to.

"So, kid. We thought you'd been stabbed, with all that blood. I've never seen anything like it except maybe in a psych ward. But even there, not this bad." He checked Harold's dressing. "What the hell got into you? You do some bad horse or acid or something?"

Harold just closed his eyes. He was so weary, and his eyelids, still edged with crisp blood, felt as heavy as the hood of a car.

"Well, you'll be out of here tomorrow, fella," the nurse said, proceeding with other duties on the other side of the narrow clinic. "Hope you don't decide to do the cat attack thing on yourself again. It's really bad for the complexion," he laughed. "Well, g' night. Sleep tight, and don't let the cat kid bite!"

The nurse turned off the light, closed the door, and locked it. Harold was relieved to be unable to stay awake. He knew what he was missing in the way of greater pain.

Harold was given a day's reprieve from his chores. The prison chaplain visited him and tried to get him to explain why he had attacked himself so viciously, but Harold couldn't answer. He might have done so, if he could have found the words, but he couldn't. He felt as if something vital had been torn from him, like an organ — his lung, heart, gut. He felt cut up, and with something cut out that couldn't be put back.

Nevertheless, he still wouldn't let his thoughts return to Jessica's letter, even though it lay bloodied on the floor by the toilet in the corner of his cell. Someone had put it there, and cleaned up most of the blood as well.

He vaguely remembered Dr. Rosenthal's letter and slowly rotated his head to the end of his bunk. It was there, still in the envelope where he had put it before reading his sister's. He was in no hurry to re-read what he thought he remembered. Rosenthal's "maybes" and "we'll sees" could wait until he could think straight and not feel. For now, he just wanted to remain on his side, knees bent and pressed up toward his chest. Movement, if he could manage it, would just stir up reality again.

Harold had been so efficient where Jessica and her feelings for him were concerned. He had let them be what he could stand them to be, and he had blocked out much of what she must have been going through. He had especially kept from his heart the fact that she could come to hate and dismiss him from her life, even though she had spoken angrily to him before and threatened to do so. He had avoided letting such a loss seep to the level of his gut. He had to try to keep renewed and re-intensified fears related to losing Jessica from flickering in his brain and heart.

The chaplain, Ben, as he asked the inmates to call him, checked on Harold again that night. He stayed on the outside and spoke softly to Harold through the chipped metal bars. Harold seemed stunned, stupefied and weathered, but still relatively youthful.

"Harold?" he whispered. Harold was sitting at the end of his cot with his hands folded across his skinny legs. He was wearing a T-shirt and jockeys, looking cold and vulnerable.

"How're you doing, kiddo? You alright?" he asked with just the right amount of concern. He didn't want Harold fearful of either of their emotions. Ben lowered himself to the floor and sat on the cement floor. He leaned against the bars that protected Harold from too much intimacy.

"Your face still looks quite a mess," he said, craning his neck to see more than part of the left side of Harold's face and head. "I see it's bruising now. Lord, young man, what were you thinking?" The chaplain regretted the last question.

Of course, Harold *hadn't* been thinking. He had reacted with such primal pain that he had attacked his external body with the same degree of primitive violence. The agony of self-hatred and guilt had swirled inside him like a self-eviscerating volcano, triggered, it would appear, by the words of probable estrangement from his sister.

Ben decided to take a risk. "Harold, you know she'll come, don't you?" He spoke softly and then waited, watching for any sign of escalating trauma. He wanted to prepare Harold for the reality of actually seeing his sister, now that she was also struggling with truth and consequences. The last thing he wanted to do, though, was to induce another episode.

"She has to say what she needs to say, son. You're her brother, and she's frightened too. She needs you to help her to understand her loss and . . . what happened." He paused. "Do you get what I mean?"

Harold's head turned ever-so-slightly sideways, and one visible, swollen eye glistened with moisture.

"Will you let her come if she asks? Come here to sort some things through?"

Still disoriented, Harold nevertheless wondered if there had been some communication between his sister and the chaplain, or his sister's shrink and the chaplain. Otherwise, how did he know about this? Had he read the letter while he was in the infirmary? He must have. Harold didn't answer.

"You'll have to at some point, Harold. Not even as much for her, even though it is the right and courageous thing to do, but for you too. You have to see her, talk to her, tell her that...

you're sorry. Do you understand?" He could no longer see Harold's eye, or even the side of his face. Harold had turned his head in silence, signaling he had shut down.

Ben remained silent for a few minutes and then rose slowly. "Gosh, that floor's hard. And cold!" he said in a slightly jocular tone, rubbing his lower back. "Let me know if you need to talk, Harold. Just let me know. I'll even be there with you if she comes, if you want. Regardless, let me know when you're ready to talk out your demons. You can't hold them inside. You just can't."

He paused, still facing Harold's back. "I'd get under those covers if I were you. You'll be a mess of goose bumps and catch cold." Ben put his hands in his pockets and sighed. "Well, goodnight son. You're in my prayers, dear boy. And so is your sister. God bless you, now."

Harold could hear the squish-squeak of the chaplain's ancient hush puppies as he walked the length of the upper level of cells. He still couldn't move.

Dr. Rosenthal's letter had said that she would try to visit him within two weeks, but that it was hard for her to get away. In a roundabout way, she reminded Harold that she wasn't his official therapist and that she would just be a visitor like anyone else.

She also mentioned his arraignment. Unbeknownst to him, he had been arraigned in absentia, something judges allowed if the defendant was in some way incapacitated or too dangerous to transfer to court for the short formality. He was officially charged with first degree murder, punishable by life imprisonment. In his case, he had already been told by the "one-in-every-prison" jailhouse lawyer that he'd no doubt serve consecutive terms — one life sentence for each life taken.

In addition to all the charges related to carrying a firearm and resisting arrest, he'd probably die in prison, or he might get lucky and be released at around 80 years old. Harold had no reaction at all to either the contents of the letter or to the free legal counseling. He knew he wouldn't make it that long.

Further, he had stopped fantasizing about anyone getting him out, especially, for some reason, after hearing from his sister. There was no one. Not his lawyer, not Rosenthal, not anyone. Who was going to risk taking a stand for *him*?

He wouldn't, he thought to himself. Just like everyone out there, *he'd* kill him if he saw him walking down the street. He'd bloody well kill him! He'd shoot himself a thousand times right in the heart for hurting his sister!

God, he hated thinking, but it kept coming back to him. Maybe if he had just thought of her, seen her, talked to her, had her crack a joke and make him laugh or, better still, if he had made *her* laugh on that day, she would still be his beautiful sister with her good life. He hadn't meant to blow away her home, her dreams. He hadn't meant to.

He started to pummel the sides of his head with his fists, and to rock back and forth, self-stimulating to distraction. He had learned that this was the most efficient way to shift from unbearable mental and emotional anguish to mere physical pain.

For all intents and purposes, Harold was back into his prison routine when he heard Dr. Rosenthal would be visiting in two days. His reaction was muted at best. He had changed so much since he had wanted her to come. He couldn't even remember why he had thought it was such a big deal.

He took the news with a combination of apathy and apprehension. He wasn't the boy she had convinced to chatter like a little moron into her stupid recorder, he thought with subdued anger. What was the point of all that? Did she think it made him feel better? Did she use it for something?

He was pretty sure she didn't listen to the tapes to relax, instead of classical music. He decided that he didn't really want to see her. What good was she? None! And who the hell was she anyway?

The only thing he might get out of it is some news about what that faggot Spencer was up to. Still nothing, he suspected. But maybe she knew something, some small bit of news — even from just reading the newspapers.

When the time came, a rutty-faced guard came to get Harold to take him to the nicer of the two visiting rooms. He wasn't as familiar with the room as most of the other prisoners were. He had only seen it once when the door had swung open to bring an inmate back to his room after a visit with his wife. He had been in line for cigarettes at the tuck shop, which was adjacent to the area, and he got a quick peek just as it was his turn to get his butts, but that was it.

Now, aware of his huge, baggy shirt and oversized work trousers, he followed the guard obediently. He licked his hand, encumbered by shackled wrists, and tried to pat down the hair on the top of his head. When they arrived, and the guard opened the door, he feigned disinterest, but tried to guess where she might be along the row of two-way cubicles separated by Plexiglas.

Two other guys were seated and leaning into the transparent barrier with old telephone receivers clutched in their huge, calloused hands, their weight balanced by threateningly taut and tattooed forearms. Visitors across from each were doing the same. He felt a shot of panic and anticipation, tinged with the surreal sound of intense, almost frantic, whispering.

Another guard in a large glass booth on the visitor's side of the long narrow room motioned him to cubicle five. He moved toward it with real effort. His instincts were to turn and run, to get back to his cell.

Funny, he thought. He recognized it as the same feeling he had when he was let out of school. He wanted to run, get past other kids, people, his parents, and be left alone in his room. Just be left alone. It was what he managed best.

The memorably pretty woman with a forced half-smile

on her face motioned Harold to sit down and pick up the receiver. She already had hers in her hand.

"Hi, Harold."

Harold rolled his eyes slightly and sat and shifted in the hard wooden chair. He reluctantly lifted the receiver from its base.

"Hi," he said insolently, looking sideways in awkward discomfort. "Th . . . thanks for coming. I guess."

Dr. Rosenthal smiled. She would have smiled at whatever he said just to ease the tension.

"What do you mean, 'I guess'?" she asked with a teasing smirk. "You wrote me to come. You practically bribed me to get myself up here!" She searched his face for a sign of humor, of connection. When he just lowered his head as if he hadn't even heard her, she proceeded, unsmiling. "How're you doing? You look awful."

For some reason, this made Harold grin, if a little painfully. He even emitted a muted chuckle, more like a snort.

"Thanks," he said, still smirking, shifting the receiver to an angle against the side of his still bruised head.

"What happened?" she asked in a tone that implied she was sure he had been beaten up as someone's Fairy Princess.

"Hurt myself. It's nothing." He lowered and turned his head again, as if he could hide the self-inflicted scars.

"It doesn't look like nothing to me. It looks as if you've been tangling with a cougar!"

This almost made him smile for real. Funny, the guard had made a cat reference too. But, of course, he was the cat.

"How've you been?" Harold asked, anxious to change the subject.

"Fine. Fine. Busy, but fine," Dr. Rosenthal responded. "But, ah, Harold, you didn't send me those tapes beggi— asking me to come out here to check on my health. What can I do for you?"

She hoped that didn't sound too formal or officious. She did give a darn about him, but knew there was little the system would allow her to contribute at this point.

"I'm sorry. I shouldn't have asked you. I was . . . confused and desperate. I thought . . . I don't know, I thought you might be able to get someone to see that I don't, or didn't, belong here or something. But that was . . . well, then."

Dr. Rosenthal slowly nodded her head, and waited pensively.

"But now I know you can't do anything and I don't mean to bother you. I just wasn't sure then of why I was here. Or I was afraid that nobody knew or cared that I was here. It's weird, and, like I said, it's different now."

"What's different?" she asked, looking both intensely curious and concerned.

"Me, I guess. And my head. I mean, I feel older or something, and I feel real bad about . . . I mean, I feel I deserve to be here now, and so what, sort of? Where would I go anyway, if someone could get me out? But no one can anyway and I shouldn't be out of here, and, I don't know, I'm probably not making much sense, but that's sort of it."

"Sort of . . . Are you saying you want to be here now, or you deserve to be here, or that you're aware of the fact that there's no one in your life with enough influence to get you out on bail, or waiting in another facility?"

She leaned forward. She sincerely wanted to understand what had changed in his inner world, no doubt due to circumstances in his restricted outer world. Her face remained close to the partition as she waited for his response.

"Yeah, I guess. All of the above. And I'm just tired. I don't think I'd move even if someone could get me in with a bunch of kids my age. I'd probably think they were pains in the ass anyway. This is okay. I mean, it's not, but it's going to have to be, right?"

Dr. Rosenthal did notice a distinct difference in Harold. He seemed lethargic and he spoke as if he were much older, someone who knew hard time. He actually sounded settled in, if that was the right phrase. She shivered imperceptibly.

"You don't actually like it here, do you?" she asked with both clinical and personal concern.

"No, I don't *like* it here, but it's some place to be. I might as well get used to it, don't ya think?"

"Why do you think that?" she asked, wondering if he had heard about the plea bargain that was probably just hours away from acceptance. She couldn't argue his point.

"Well, other stuff aside and all, why do you think I'm here? For throwing marbles in the schoolyard?"

"Harold, you don't have to be sarcastic, or talk down to me. What's changed? Why have you . . . given up? Or, I don't know, resigned yourself to—"

"To what?" Harold interrupted. "Life in prison? Gee, I don't know. It just came to me as a good idea one night when I was brushing my teeth in the toilet, or when some big ape who kills people for fun pulled my dick in the shower. Maybe it was when a guard propositioned me and told me he could make my life easier if I just blew him off a few times a week! I don't know!"

Dr. Rosenthal straightened her purse and gloves in front of her as if she were about to leave. Harold obviously wasn't going to divulge anything. He was no doubt unable to understand or explain his apparently sudden resignation. There seemed little point in dragging this out. She had to get back to her office for a session.

"Okay, okay. I guess it's none of my business, Harold. I just had the silly notion that if I drove all the way up here, at your request I might add, there might be something you wanted to tell or ask me. Call me crazy. I thought you wanted to talk." She started to rise from her chair, lowering the receiver as she did.

"Have you heard anything?" Harold mumbled. Dr. Rosenthal didn't have the receiver to her ear, so she didn't hear, but she saw the faintest sign of panic in Harold's eyes. "Have I what?" She lowered herself to the chair again.

"Have you heard anything? About me, the trial, what my damn lawyer's doing, or whether I'm just going to live here for the rest of my life without it being made official or anything? Sort of like forced living in a filthy condo full of perverted mental cases?!"

Evidently, he hadn't heard. He hadn't either been asked or informed. Again, Dr. Rosenthal was furious, but she tried to keep her anger in check. She wasn't even sure she should be telling him anything.

"There . . . there are things going on, Harold." She paused, trying to make a flash decision as to whether to put herself in potentially hot water. Her professionalism kept her from making uninformed, rash decisions most of the time and she couldn't see anything wrong with telling him. Someone should have told him already. Someone also should have counseled him as to his options, as limited as they were. Harold interrupted her thinking.

"Like what? A state or nationwide plan for a festive lynching? I know everyone wants me dead. I'm too scary. I was too scary for them even before I did it. Everyone wants everyone else to be normal, easy, and to say the same old right things all the time. Any difference and you're dead — one way or another. So, screw 'em. What're they deciding to do with the freak?"

She appeared to ignore his short speech. "There are talks going on to . . . well, to make an agreement with the state, the prosecutor's office, and to avoid a trial. I—"

Harold cut her off again, snorted loudly and slapped his knee. "See, they want to make it easy, and trying a kid who kills kids ain't easy, is it? It'd make all the perfect, normal people puke! Damn cowards! So, what 're they going to do, just vote on how to kill me?"

"No, Harold, killing you isn't in the discussion."

"It isn't? Oh, thank God, because I've never wanted to miss a second of life and, well, since this all went down, I, as people say, 'cherish' life more than ever!" He placed his hand on his heart and raised his eyes in mock inspiration.

Dr. Rosenthal was becoming increasingly frustrated, partly because she wasn't his legal advisor and really didn't feel comfortable giving him news he should already have from another source. But she knew Bob Spencer didn't like confrontation or controversy. He liked to be the white knight on the right side of things, and he wasn't that great with people. She'd known that he would do as little communicating as possible with this client. He didn't want the association professionally, nor did he want to have to face and deal with hostility at the country club.

"They're talking about . . . second degree murder. That is, second degree murder with the maximum sentence for each child and for each of your . . . parents."

Harold looked at her. "And what's the maximum for whatever second degree murder is?" he asked with a tone that sounded as if he were arguing or negotiating his own terms.

"Second degree murder assumes that there were extenuating circumstances, and that you didn't, in theory or otherwise, actually plan to . . . to . . . do what you did. It assumes that you were in a state of mind that affected your judgement. The . . . the maximum sentence is twenty-five to life."

Dr. Rosenthal watched his face for a reaction. He was rotating the receiver so that the mouthpiece was now above his head. "That's assuming you're never paroled."

After a long moment of what seemed like calm distraction, he asked, "For each? Life for each?"

"Yes. Twenty-five to life for each."

"So, like, forever, right? I mean, even with good behavior, I'd be a skeleton before I ever got out of here, right?"

"You'd be . . . much older. Yes." She had lowered her head and now raised it again. "And you can't assume you'll stay here. You might be moved to a maximum-security facility in another state. It could even be a, well, a more crowded and challenging environment."

Harold looked at her incredulously, and then burst into laughter. It rose to virtual hysterics. She was taken aback and confused by his outburst. She watched him with annoyance for a minute before she interrupted.

"Harold, what's so damn funny? Harold? Are you okay? Harold!" She yelled his name and hit the partition with her purse.

The guard in the cubicle who had been reading peacefully, looked up and strained his neck to make sure everything was alright. Dr. Rosenthal looked over at him and smiled with embarrassment.

"Challenging." Harold smiled, then laughed some more, his face contorted. "A more 'challenging' environment! I love it. You don't know about challenge, lady! Challenging!" He yelled the word at the top of his lungs, sharing her choice of words with the entire room, and again, drawing the attention of the increasingly vigilant guard.

In fact, the duty guard must have signaled Harold's prison escort because the same pocked-faced guard reappeared while Harold was still in what seemed to be semi-hysterics. He had just laid his head down and enveloped it in his arms when the guard grabbed his elbow.

Dr. Rosenthal noticed that Harold didn't so much as tighten up under the grip. He was used to being removed from situations and environments without warning. Time was always in someone else's control.

"Bye, Harold," Sandra half-called as he was turned side-

ways and yanked upward to leave. "Take care." Then, upset by
the abrupt end of their visit, as well as by the unsettling nature
of it, as an afterthought, she yelled, "Phone Spencer. You have
a right to hear how it comes out as soon as possible. Phone
him, Harold!"

Dr. Rosenthal didn't know how to feel when she heard
Harold joking in a monologue about the fact that he might be
going to a more "challenging" facility. She felt stupid, as if she
had been of no use or help to him, but she felt something else
as well. She felt as if she had just spent time with a mad, but
wise, old man. She felt inept and somehow mentally reduced
and scrambled. She needed to shake off the composite of feelings that suddenly made it difficult for her to think or focus.
She needed to straighten up, get back to work, and then get
home to feed the kids.

When she had finally passed through the five sliding metal
doors preceded by checkpoints and virtual frisking, she found
herself outdoors, immediately conscious of the elevated, rifle-
toting guards watching her from behind their dark glasses.

She felt a kind of panic and wanted to get to her car as
quickly as possible, but she couldn't remember where she had
parked it. She had been told exactly where she could leave it,
but that seemed like days ago, and now she didn't have a clue
where it was. It even took her a minute to remember which
car she had driven.

Increasingly uncomfortable under the intense gaze of the
guards, she just kept moving and hoped that she was heading
in the general direction of visitor parking. She didn't want to
appear to be wandering.

An innocuously faint and civilized voice in her told her
to calm down, that she was a taxpayer and a professional, and
she had a right to be here as a visitor. Another voice, more
like an indescribable scream from a place deep within her, made
her heart pound and prodded her to run for her life. Again,

she tried to appear normal and was struck by the fact that she had no idea what "normal behavior" would or should be under the circumstances.

TWELVE

Done Deals Done

Harold DIDN'T THINK the way he used to before killing, before being anally searched, courted by big, older guys who wanted him to be their "wife," being regularly beaten for being in the wrong place at the wrong time.

Maybe he thought and felt badly about the visit with Dr. Rosenthal. But he didn't really. He did, however, think enough to think it strange that he didn't care enough to think about it much at all. He knew he had been rude, hostile, even grossly ungrateful with her, but he didn't care. It wasn't as if he'd be suspended or anything, plus the tentative connection he had felt for her had thinned considerably.

He had felt like a foreigner talking to her, but she was actually the foreigner. He felt blocked and resentful. She had wanted to be so receptive and supportive, but he knew that was fine in theory, but a joke in practice. How could she fathom what he needed? *He* didn't even know.

Further, how could she fathom what his life had become? And it *had* become his life. He was defined by where he was, how smoothly his duties went, whether he got through the

day without any serious or injurious trouble. He was, theoretically, a kid in an adult's hell, but he didn't feel like a kid anymore. From the inside-out he had, within months, gone from
a terrified little creep impressed with guns, listening to heavy
metal alone in his room, to an inmate in the modern equiva-
lent of a dungeon.

The only difference from a real dungeon and the prison
was, instead of it being surrounded by a moat filled with alli-
gators, he was in a cell in a stone building, behind four-foot-
thick and twenty-foot-high walls trimmed with barbed wire
and manned by guards armed with automatic machine guns
just itching to pop someone off.

How could "Dr. Sandra Rosenthal" possibly help or even
relate to him now? Anything she'd have to say at this point
would sound like the theme song for a Brady Bunch rerun.
That day she had sounded distanced and muddled and the
visit was less than useless from Harold's perspective. It con-
firmed that there was no adult in the world who could do anything for him, even understand him and his new non-life.

He was a con, a lifer. He had the glazed, protectively emotionless eyes of his new species. He also had the reflexive sus-
picion of connections and the mental and emotional retrac-
tion that comes with an absence of hope.

Two days later, he received another piece of confirming
information, though this time it didn't come via a visitor. Dr.
Rosenthal was right. Bob Spencer hadn't called, but he had
sent a very fancy letter at which Harold had to smirk as he
read. It said, amid all the camouflaging legal mumbo jumbo,
that a deal had been struck, and that his lawyer was "pleased
to tell him" that he would not be on death row, but rather in
prison for the rest of his life.

Harold wondered if he should hold a cell party. The letter went on to state the one stipulation attached to the sentencing agreement. He had to write an allocution — that is,

he had to go through, action by action, detail by detail —
what he had done that day, the day of the shootings. He was
to spare nothing, and a judge would deem whether or not his
descriptive admission and remorse were sufficient.

The mere thought of really remembering, reliving, or just
giving a superficial version of the events, made Harold sick.
Perverts, he thought. They just can't wait to have a record of
how a kid kills — as if the details of that day would tell them
anything.

He didn't even know why or how he did what he did, or
even how long it took! He hadn't dared think back to shooting his mom or his dad. The first month, he had thought of his
mom often. He even awoke in a sweat, calling out to her. He
certainly hadn't really wanted her dead, so how the hell were
they going to get anything useful out of his telling them a
scary story that wasn't the real story anyway?

He had hoped, months back, to work some things out
with Rosenthal, but the system wouldn't allow for it. He guessed
all they wanted was a teary-eyed description of blood, screams
and tears.

They wanted it verbalized or, in his case, he was informed,
written and witnessed as an affidavit to be submitted to the
court. What he wrote, he thought bitterly, would be his life,
how he would be forever remembered, except for the fact that
five years from now, the story would include something like
chewing rat heads before the fact and taking out six police
officers before he was arrested.

The chain story would inevitably evolve further to include screwing live or dead animals – anything to ensure that
the thrill of community horror was kept alive as an even uglier suburban legend than it already was. He would be the new
stalker-killer with the hooked hand, the monster in the best
ghost story of the new millennium.

Then what would happen to him?

It was just one day they wanted him to spill his guts over, to paint an ugly picture of what happened, incomplete and without a frame, as if he had never existed before the incident. Yet, ironically, Harold himself knew or felt that, in a way, he hadn't. In an odd way, he had an identity, a persona and a place where he belonged for the first time in his life.

It took four phone calls and then a more than mildly threatening letter before Harold forced himself to take five minutes here and five minutes there, to write his allocution. While he tried to remain detached, he also had to try to do a decent job.

He didn't think he could do it twice without losing it. What did they think? That he didn't love his parents? That he thought killing kids was funny? That he did it because he thought it was the cool thing to do? He wanted to get it right the first time, but stay sufficiently in control not to shit his pants. He couldn't afford to become vulnerable or go around looking scared, pensive, or upset. He had learned to appear as "in your face," as cold and uncaring as possible.

Harold was now fifteen going on fifty. He knew the older and meaner he looked, and the less reaction he showed anyone about anything, the safer he was. He had reached a milestone just a few days before when he stepped over a stabbed body in the shower as if he were stepping over a discarded towel. The thing was still pulsing and gushing blood. Someone had gotten the poor stiff in the neck, the target of choice, probably over a pack of butts or a hit of cocaine. Harold knew better than to see or speak evil. Later in the day, he served who he knew to be the stabber and gave him extra scoops of thick, rich, red tomato sauce with his spaghetti. Luckily, the guy didn't get it. He just thought Harold was sucking up, which was partly true.

Ben helped him with the document. The experience left him shaken, but okay, and now he shifted to waiting for word as to whether his admission and description to the court was sufficiently "inclusive." While he was trying to preoccupy himself in his routine, Harold got more upsetting news.

Jessica *was* coming to see him. Again, he could say no, but this was precisely why it was such a mind screw up. He didn't want to see her, especially so soon after having to focus, albeit as emotionlessly as possible, on what he had done. But he felt he owed her.

Harold didn't want to face her for many reasons he had already been through in his head a hundred times. How could *she* want to unless she was going to try to sneak a pistol in to blow his brains out through the Plexiglas? He knew she had come to hate him enough to do it. She had said as much.

So, why come? Why would she *want* to see him? How could she stand to lay eyes on him? He hated even thinking about it, but he had to make a decision. He felt damned if he did, and damned if he didn't. He wasn't sure *he* could stand to see *her*. This was no time. There would never be a time for falling apart. The decision kept him awake and tore him into emotional shreds.

Ben had been back about it, ministering outside his cell again, trying to convince him that he owed it to Jessica, that it was for her and not for him, that he had to find the courage to face her again for her sake. He also preached the benefits Harold could expect from the sense of redemption he would feel when he saw and felt that he was still her little brother, and still had a connection on the outside.

Harold thought Ben must be a bit out of touch with reality. He couldn't see any good coming out of this for him. Maybe for her, on some theoretical, psychological level, but not for *him*. He needed to stay numb and blank, not to remember or feel connections.

Harold was still struggling with both the decision and re-ignited emotions when Ben told him something that made things even more complicated and difficult. It had been Jessica pushing the lawyer to get her brother's case dealt with and closed. She had forked out some money to hire Spencer an assistant and to pay for a few other bits of expensive legal work.

She had also been the one to argue that he be allowed to describe his crime on paper so as to avoid a public appearance, more dramatic and humiliating pictures on the front page of the local paper, and a gawking, public hate born partly of a love of good gore. Unbeknownst to anyone but her, Spencer, the judge and her therapist, she had also heard that at least two of the fathers of the dead children had sworn to kill him and were just waiting for his and their day in court. She had fought for his relative safety.

Jessica was stable enough to know that Harold was as safe where he was as he would ever be. In this way, his sentence was merciful. Even if the system *had* tried to help him, to understand and help him, he could never have returned to society unless he changed his name and moved to another continent. Even then, he would eventually be uncovered or found out. Like an old Nazi, someday, sometime, he'd be shot in the head, executed as a killer of kids. He would always, until the day he died, be the boy who killed his parents and schoolmates – most memorably, the latter.

Feeling as if he had no choice, Harold agreed, but only for two weeks down his monotonous road. He needed to prepare himself, as if he could. He also wanted time to back out, and for her to be able to do the same. For this, he had room to hope.

During the week before the now scheduled visit, Harold was beaten up four times, blocked by inmates from using the central shower for three days, and had a five gallon pot of steaming hot chili thrown at him at the meal counter. It stuck to him like napalm and would leave him scarred with second-degree burns.

He also got into a handful of fights, primarily because he wasn't as alert. At times, it was as if he were asking for it, being foolish and taking risks that could only lead to trouble. He not only carried the scent of vulnerability, he seemed to need the pain, the punishment that was so easy to come by in an environment where cause and violent effect were both reflexive and clear.

However, whether consciously or unconsciously, the abuse Harold brought upon himself did nothing to allay the mounting, burning guilt he felt at the mere memory of Jessica's face. He had felt guilt anyway, all along, once he fully realized what he had done, but this was different. She was his own sister, he had adored her, and she'd come in from the outside where he had left her with nothing, not even a home she could go back to because of what he had done there.

She was coming to see him, to look at him, to work something through by speaking to him. He wished and wished, even willed her to turn her anger into hatred and rejection, to come to find him so vile that she couldn't bear the sight of him. His greatest need was for her to stay away from the person he had become. He didn't understand what her need was, and, compared to his, didn't really care. He sure as hell didn't need redemption.

What the hell was he going to do with it? Open a school for wayward, lost, exploding kids? He was in prison for life, for God's sake. Why did he need to get any better, feel any better, even breathe deeply, for that matter? It didn't make sense – no sense at all.

Like virtually all things from the outside, it just didn't work for him. It was all an actionable cliche, like the impossible, but urgent essence of one of his sister's books, *The Road Less Traveled*, where the first line is, "Life is difficult."

It's not just difficult, he thought to himself, it's lethal, and assholes make it worse by writing dangerously simple things

about how to do life "easier." He imagined his sister reading
all kinds of books on forgiveness and such, when there were
times when someone should just be strung up by the balls.

He didn't sleep. He couldn't. He was in such a sweat that
he must have wiped his armpits a hundred times in four hours.
He kept looking in the rubber and plastic mirror to see whether
he was recognizable. He tried to get as much light as possible
from the dim, fluorescent fixture outside and at an angle from
his cell.

He didn't think she'd recognize him. He felt and thought
he looked bigger, uglier, harder — just the way a murderer
should look. The mask he wore to deal with prison life had
merged with his skull and face, becoming more and more real.
He wasn't anybody's kid brother anymore. He was an inmate,
an under-grounder, a professional low-life.

He could barely see any signs of who he had been and
what he had looked like. His brown eyes had grown darker
and one eyebrow was slightly thicker than another. He had
learned to tighten his full lips under what were now slightly, if
permanently flared, narrow nostrils.

He wished he had developed a cleft chin, but unlike the
sudden growth of facial hair, it hadn't happened and probably
wouldn't. However, he had already decided he would get one.
He had watched an inmate give himself one in the shower
with a Popsicle stick unevenly broken in half. The guy just
gouged it into his chin. It had bled for about three days and
then scabbed and left an uneven scar that passed just fine for a
cleft. In addition to the rougher things Harold was learning in
prison, he was learning a rustic form of cosmetic surgery.

In terms of recognizing who he had been, Harold knew
what to look past and through. In addition to what he had
developed in the way of layers of protection, there was something shared in common in the face, especially the eyes of
every inmate. They were all slow to blink, seemed to be in a

permanent squint and carried with them the alertness of preda-
tor and prey.

He had little memory of what he had looked like before.
He had never really looked. He knew how others had looked
at him, how they had reacted, and he hadn't ever figured out
what they were sneering at or rejecting. He wondered if he
were to see an old picture of himself whether he would recognize himself. He doubted it.

A guard's bat hit a bar at the far, upper left corner of his
cell. The loud clang and reverberation shook his cot and Harold
reflexively threw himself to the floor. He thought someone
had gotten a hold of a gun or a metal pipe and was going on a
rampage before lunch.

His ears were still ringing when the guard stopped snickering over Harold's hyper-vigilant reaction. He felt a deeper
and worse fear, then a stab to his gut and ringing in his ears
when the guard told him he had a visitor.

"Mighty pretty young thing, Harold m' boy. Mighty pretty
indeed. Says she's your sister," the guard added with real or
mocking skepticism. He unlocked the cell and raised his arm
to signal Harold that he was coming out whether he wanted
to or not. "C'mon now, let's not keep the gal waiting. She
come all this way to see her killer brother. Beats me why, but
she's here, all dressed up and all. So, let's go. C'mon, kid!"

He cuffed Harold's wrists and chained his ankles. The
latter was traditional, yet discretionary, prison policy. It depended on the guard, the day, the mood in the prison, all sorts
of things. It was the major unpredictable for most inmates,
most of which related to individual temperaments and territo-
rial or proprietary flare-ups.

There were also prison politics involving the inmates and
guards alike. Amid the structure and repetition of prison life,
where there were no variables, it was the one thing they learned
to live with. Harold, however, learned to just extend his wrists

and spread his legs whenever he was called from his cell for anything but his duties. The policy seemed to be mandatory – at least for him.

Today, he found the customized short-step walk particularly difficult given his level of panic and nausea. The guard kept pushing him from behind, which didn't make maintaining his balance any easier. He fell twice, reflexively falling on his side, while protecting his elbow.

It was called the "chain fall" and he had learned it early on, as if it were a gymnastic move. If one didn't pick it up quickly, one could smash one's face, break a rib, or even shatter an elbow. He pretty well had it down pat.

They arrived and he dug deep within himself for some undefined brand of strength. At the same time, he inhaled enough air to push his chest out and look up. After all, he didn't have a choice. He could at least try not to look as if he were being pushed around like somebody's beat up dog.

At first, he couldn't see her. He was looking and pretending not to, so he looked harder, thinking he must not be focusing intensely enough, but when he did a full pan of the other side of the visiting room, she was nowhere to be seen.

He was just beginning to wonder if the guard was messing with him, or if she had decided she didn't want to see him and had left, when there was some movement at the visitor's entrance. There she was.

The guard was letting her in as she apologized for inconveniencing him. Harold wouldn't have known what had gone on except that the guard, obviously finding his sister attractive and thinking he was ingratiating himself with her, said, "No worry. No worry. When you have to go, you have to go!" He punctuated his flirtatious rendition with a conspiratorial giggle, a couple of winks and a quick pat to the middle of Jessica's back.

She just smiled shyly, and, head down, moved toward the

seat where Harold saw she had already placed her sweater. She had been crying. She also looked frightened and stiff, as if she herself were wearing a starched prison suit, was chained, and had her face pressed behind and against an invisible mask. Just as Harold was thinking how he couldn't blame her for being tense and afraid, she looked up and saw him.

Her face betrayed her shock. As much as she tried to receive him unflinchingly, Harold could see that much registered when she looked at him. The incident, the losses, her own inner torture, the way he looked, all came together in her eyes meeting his.

He stood, paralyzed, until the guard became impatient and pushed him toward where he would sit across from her. They hadn't yet unlocked eyes and even after Harold sat down, they continued to stare at each other, as if that was all each of them needed to do.

Almost surprising himself, Harold was first to slowly raise his hand to the telephone receiver. He wouldn't have thought he'd have it in him, but the process, whatever it was, had to start somewhere with someone. By the time Harold had the device to his ear, his sister had reached for the one on her side of the clear barrier. It was almost a toss up as to who actually spoke first.

"Hi," Harold said softly, looking away right after he said it. He felt the burning again, and the nausea and panic. He wanted to run rather than look into his sister's beautiful, but contorted face.

"Hi, H. How's it going . . . in here?" she asked tentatively.

No one had called him "H" for as long as he could remember. She gave him that nickname when he was born and had always said it ebulliently when she phoned from university and he answered, or during Christmas or his birthday. It always made him feel kind of good for some reason.

"It's going," he answered, still distracted by thoughts of nice moments gone.

"You look, well, a little sick or something. Are you sick, H?" she asked, examining his face and neck, up and down, and trying to get a look at his ears. She thought he looked incredibly old, at least three times his age.

"I'm not sick. I . . . I'm okay. Really, I'm okay."

They both knew there was so much to say, but so little they actually dared to put into words. They sat for a full minute or two, Jessica looking at him as if to find a clue to a mystery, and Harold looking everywhere but at his sister.

"How're the Andersons?" Harold finally asked. They were the family Jessica was staying with. They had been really good to her after she came back.

"They're fine. They've been terrific. But if I stay any longer, I'm going to insist on paying something for room and board." She lowered her head, remembering that she hadn't told them she was seeing Harold. They wouldn't have approved.

They knew she was seeing a psychiatrist who encouraged her to confront the brother she had loved so much, but they thought the therapist was a quack. They didn't say as much, but it was pretty clear that's how they felt.

"Well, I bet they send their regards to me, huh?" Harold snorted. Then he paused and looked up. "Jamie was there that day, wasn't he?" Jamie was their son.

"Ah, well, they probably wonder how you are. I'm sure they do," Jessica answered uncomfortably. "And Jamie? Yes, he was there, but he was practicing hoops in the gym, so he was, well, safe and got out from the back before —"

"Before I started to massacre anything that moved, right?" Harold interrupted her and looked her right in the eye. She looked away, to the side, and bit her lower lip.

"Lucky little prick, wasn't he? I wonder if they'd let you stay there if I'd killed him. I wonder, good Christian folk that they are," he added sarcastically.

She looked at him again. "What're you doing talking like that? Are you trying to shock me, or what? What does that really stupid statement, or question, or whatever it was, mean, Harold?!"

She looked as if her camouflage was melting, exposing a primitive fury. Her color grew higher, her eyes more intense. Veins in her neck and forehead stuck out, pulsating. Harold noticed that the old "H" was gone. He also realized that he had been a smart ass and had gotten them into dangerous territory.

"I just meant that, well, it's great that he's okay, I guess. I don't know. It wasn't anything heavy or anything," he said, sounding defensive, but knowing he deserved her reaction.

"Nothing heavy!" she hissed, shaking her head. "No, there's nothing 'heavy' about your kid almost getting killed by a schoolmate and child of your friends! Nothing at all!"

Harold looked down, feeling both contrite and incredibly stupid. He also felt shame. Strangely enough, the shame wasn't as much over what he had done, as it was over how his sister was looking and talking to him. She had always treated him like an equal and said he had potential and told him he'd be fine if he was just patient and let himself grow up. Now here she was, wanting, he suspected, to jump over the glass and strangle him. There was silence again.

Harold did his best to change the subject. He would have preferred to just leave and go back to the comfortable emptiness of his cell, but he tried to be pleasant. "What's going to happen with university and all? You going back?" he asked as if they had just finished discussing the weather. He already knew the answer.

She gave him a disconcerted look before answering. "I don't know what I'm going to do! I think you can probably imagine that this . . . this mess has kind of thrown me off a bit. Can you imagine that, Harold?" Her tone was tight, tough and sarcastic. He wasn't going to get her back. Of course he could imagine, but he didn't know what to say.

"Yeah, I guess. I mean, of course. I didn't mean to. . . ."

"You didn't mean to what, Harold? Kill them? Mom and Dad and a bunch of innocent kids? You didn't *mean* to?" She dropped her head into her free hand. "Well, that makes me feel a whole hell of a lot better! Really, it does!"

Even though he knew he deserved it, and had thought this might happen, Harold felt defenseless. What could he do? He wasn't about to try to figure out everything right now with her.

Part of him wished they could talk about some of it, but he realized that was unrealistic given the fact that they hadn't seen each other in so long, and had each been evolving separately in new environments with new challenges. Bottom line was that he *had* done what he had done, and that everyone, including his sister, was effectively gone.

He tried to respond. "I mean, I didn't plan or anything. I didn't want to do it," he answered almost plaintively.

She looked back at him as if she were about to spit. He had never seen her look so angry, almost grotesque. "Oh, so who made you do it, Harold? Who? Did the devil make you do it? Did some voice come down from on high and say, 'Shoot Mom in the throat while she makes your damn toast'?! Why the hell did you do it?!"

She realized she had raised her voice. She lowered it to an angry, wet whisper. "Who are you, anyway? Who the hell gave you the right to kill my parents and then go on some B.B. gun rampage with an automatic rifle?! Did you think you were God for a day?! What?! Tell me, Harold! Tell me why this happened!"

She was trying to hold back tears, but her eyes were filling up and overflowing. They had the drawn glistening look of the eyes of a wounded animal, still raging, but instinctively giving up.

"I can't answer that," he whispered, turning sideways in his chair. There was a pause, but before she could jump on him, he added, "I don't understand. Something just took me out of myself or something. Something made me want to not live another day as a piece of ignorable, useless piece of dirt. I just didn't want to live another frigging, lousy day. That's all I know. All I can say." He had his hand over his forehead now, and was pressing the earpiece against his jaw.

"Why . . . why didn't you just. . . ?"

"Kill myself? I know, that's what my lawyer said too, and the prosecutor, and the sheriff, and the cops, and everyone who's talking and writing about what I did as if they have the smallest clue of what was going on with me!

"I don't even know what was going on with me, but everyone seems to know and everyone says I should have just swallowed the gun myself and left everyone else alone!"

He forced his eyes to turn hard, just so that they wouldn't soften and allow for the flow of tears. "I should've. I know. But it wasn't as if I was clear about what I was doing or anything. I didn't make a list and whip it out one morning intending to kill people, like . . . Mom and Dad. If I had known this was going to happen, I would've offed myself right in the damn basement! Then everything would be just fine for everyone!"

Jessica wasn't sympathetic. She needed an explanation that worked for her, inside her, in a place where she was dealing with her own struggle. Realistic or rational or not, she couldn't leave without *something* to help her to understand.

"Were you or had you been doing drugs?" she asked, trying to sound a bit more sympathetic in order to get a truthful answer.

Harold had crossed his arms and lowered his head. He wasn't looking at her. He wasn't looking at or seeing anything, even though his eyes appeared to be open. He was imagining killing himself. He didn't mean to go there in his mind, but he slid into that place or dimension where things seem real, but aren't.

It was like one of those dreams he had had before when he was sure, even though he knew he was dreaming, that what was happening was real. He let this one — this experience of blowing his brains out — go on and on, until he had blown what was left of his torso across the basement walls. Headless, thoughtless, emotionless, and as still as a bloody doll without a face laying propped against the old furnace, he could smell his own corpse.

He smiled, pleased with the result of his imagined re-doing and undoing of that day.

"I guess that means you were, or you aren't going to tell me if you were." Jessica's anger re-flared. She couldn't figure out who her brother had become and why he seemed to show no feeling at all for their parents, the children, or her. She prided herself on the marks she had earned in her psychology courses, but they weren't helping her to understand her brother's actions.

Further, Jessica was a mess herself. She knew how long the medication she had taken before coming in would last. Its effects were starting to wear thin enough that she thought she might lose it — scream at him, cry uncontrollably as she had for weeks, have a massive panic attack and run around scream-ing like a mad woman.

She'd had one just the day before in the grocery store with Mrs. Anderson and almost didn't come today. Poor Mrs. Anderson. Jessica was convinced that, for a moment there, the middle-aged woman thought she was going to pull a "Harold." She apologized later and tried to explain the attacks the way her psychiatrist had explained them to her. Mrs. Ander-son had just nodded her head and then made tea. Jessica vowed never to have another attack, especially in front of the Andersons.

"Well, Harold," Jessica started, taking a deep breath and exhaling slowly, consciously counting down from ten to one. "You clearly have nothing you want or need to say to me. I'm really, really glad I came! I have such a better understanding of everything now! How could I have been so dumb not to understand what you've so eloquently cleared up for me? I've been such a dunce!"

Her sarcasm not only dripped, it virtually misted the partition. She started to gather her things. Harold had slowly lifted his head, not hearing, but watching while she spoke. Now, he watched with a hint of dismay, fear, and sadness combined as she rustled in her purse for keys and wiped her eyes with a Kleenex.

He had a vague sense of her turning snow white, and breathing as if she had been running to catch up to something, but didn't know what it was, or when to stop. He couldn't say anything. The receiver lay on the table at his side. She had put hers in the holder.

"Bye, Harold," she mouthed, turning only slightly. She uttered "little bastard" under her breath as she strutted toward and then virtually pounded on the guard's door to be let out. She smiled with forced calm, waiting for the torpid official to hear her over his transistor radio.

Finally, the guard looked at her and then at Harold. He wondered if he had missed something and why the visit was being cut short. She looked okay, if upset. The kid prisoner was just sitting there, staring, as if someone had shot him with a stun gun. There certainly wasn't any apparent danger or aggression in his eyes or body.

On the contrary, he looked dead, as if his body or life system had been turned off, and as if, were someone to touch him, he'd just fall loosely to the floor. The guard buzzed Jessica out into the exit hall, and then radioed his colleague to collect Harold and take him back to his cell.

When the escorting guard arrived, he quickly became irritated with Harold's lassitude. If he didn't know better, that is, that it was impossible to get past the checkpoints with contraband, the guard would have thought the kid's pretty little sister had brought him some dope.

The kid couldn't or wouldn't move his damn legs. He was as limp as a dead body. Luckily for Harold, the guard didn't hit him, and only pushed him so that he fell to the cement floor twice before a colleague came along and agreed to help out. Two hefty guards dragged Harold and chatted about their Wednesday night poker game, as if they were merely hauling produce. Because he was heavy and awkward to lift and pull, they had to stop periodically to adjust their grips. He seemed like an unidentifiable, dead mammal – deaf, dumb, and slotted to a storage pen just far enough away for the two older men to resent the work required to get him there.

The guards half-plopped him on the cot and the floor, deciding enough was enough. "I think he's forgotten how to walk with all that cheap jewelry," one guard said to his associate, motioning to the ankle chains. They left, making arrangements about their poker game later that night.

They were referring, of course, to Harold's shackles. And they were half-right. The chains around Harold's ankles scraped the floor as he tried to move so that the edged, metal bar on his cot wasn't cutting into his flesh. However, his feet were no more cooperative than his chained and banded arms and wrists which the guards had neglected to remove, and would leave on for another hour before returning.

It was as if he could no longer control his body or get it to work, as if he were headless, immobile, and capable of only the bluntest of images, bereft of real thought. He wasn't even aware of the added weight and restriction of external chains.

THIRTEEN

Manageable Outcomes

FOUR DAYS LATER, Harold remained unable and unwilling to leave his cell. He had been dragged out twice to eat, but he wouldn't. Nor could he perform any of the duties that had become part of his routine. In spite of the array of emotions, even strange mental states Harold had experienced in his time, he had never before been as stuck and stupefied as he was with the apparent loss of his connection with his sister. The face-to-face reality of her contempt, and her final abandonment of him, were beyond what he could bear. Nor, however, could he bear what he had done to her to force her to leave him.

He got away with it, though he was shouted at, threatened, and twice manhandled by frustrated guards. Things had been made more complex by the fact that he was not only silent and immobile, but he had developed a prodigious nosebleed right after the visit. No matter what he did or didn't do, it wouldn't stop. It was as if he, as a mechanism, had seized up. Yet, paralysed, he was pumping and pulsating like a pressure cooker spitting hot blood.

The guards became sick of getting bloodied every time they tried to get him up and functioning. He had been sent to the infirmary on the evening of the second day and his nostrils had been stretched and packed, but when he awoke from a sedative the next day, the bleeding hadn't stopped. If anything, it was worse. The warden was being kept apprised and there were discussions by prison officials as to whether to send him into the city hospital for treatment.

Harold wasn't complaining, though. One always relatively decent guard noticed he was getting pale and that he still, after three more days, wasn't moving from one position on his bed. He asked him if he was feeling weak, if he was alright. Harold didn't answer; rather, he just lay staring at the ceiling. He held a bloody, prison issue washcloth against his face as if it were an oxygen mask, and his own blood was the filter through which he breathed to stay alive. Both hands were bloody from switching to hold the cloth in place. His loose hand lay beside him balled into a fist.

He appeared to be either squeezing, trapping his own blood in his hand as some kind of reminder or punishment, or he was holding it, keeping it warm, as if protecting it. He also continued to lie in it, and dried blood formed crusted, brown-red lines down either side of his face. Another guard joked that Harold was going "psycho" on them, that he liked the blood, and that's why it didn't stop, but even *his* laughter was somewhat forced. None of the guards had ever seen anything like it – all this blood with no apparent penetration of the flesh.

Luckily, he had loads of time to rest. He was now being left alone and no one had called, not even his lawyer to tell him a deal had been worked out. Spencer probably figured his sister had told him. Technically, the manner in which Spencer was handling the case posed possible grounds for an appeal, but everyone was pretty sure that Harold was in no shape to do jailhouse lawyering. They were right — he just wanted to be left alone to bleed, or to stop bleeding, or to die from the loss of what was essential to living. No one was sure. Luckily the prison doctor had finally instructed the warden that he was to remain still until the bleeding stopped. Now his rest was official — the first strategic institutional move in his favor.

It was day six when it happened. Lucky for most of the few kinder guards, none of them were on their shift when the news came in. In fact, the guards on duty first heard about it on the old transistor radio they listened to at one of the checkpoints. They heard something about a car crash that seemed suspicious – some car running out of control right into a brick wall. They were hooting about how someone could lose control in an empty parking lot and drive into a wall. The driver was reported dead, the report said, and was part of a "larger community story."

Jessica Connally was the name of the identified body. When one of the guards recognized the name, he hushed the others and turned up the volume. He wasn't sure, but he thought the killer kid on upper level B had had a visit from a sister named Jessica. The only reason it clicked was that a few of the guards had been going on about what a hot number she was. Now she was dead, if it was her.

Even for hardened prison staff, this was rough stuff. The small group fell silent. They, like everyone else in the country, knew the story, and two of them had dealt for some time with Harold. They couldn't help feeling sick. They couldn't believe, even with all the stuff they had seen and heard over the years, how much could go wrong from one pinpoint of human life. God, who was going to tell him?

None of them wanted the job. They'd wait 'til morning and let Bull do it.

Bull didn't mind being called the vernacular name for a

prison guard, which was usually, ironically given his overt masculinity, the name for a female prison guard in a female prison. He was a big guy, African American, very efficient, and no nonsense, but never mean unless he had to be.

He had previously been a boxer before he got sick of having his nose smashed in and having dizzy spells. If he had to, or was forced, he could rip an inmate's shoulder out of its socket with two fingers, or knock down the largest inmate with a flash of his fist. *He* could tell Harold, his colleagues hoped. He could do it without much ado. Just get it done. He had a way with things that were sensitive, even though he was a man of few words, and much bulk. They'd let him know when he came on his shift at 4:00 A.M. Meanwhile, they'd also try to track Ben, who was on a four-day leave.

Night and morning overlapped for Bull as he prepared for work. His colleagues would find that he had already heard what they were stewing about, awaiting his arrival. It was all over the morning papers. **"KID KILLER'S SISTER SUS-PECTED OF TAKING OWN LIFE!"** It was also on all the radio, TV channels, and all the talk at gas stations, coffee joints and anything else open for night workers or their early morning relief.

On his regular drive to work, Bull usually sang choruses from the Baptist hymns he enjoyed so much with his family at church on Sundays. This morning, he drove in silence. Whether it was due to the absence of his own voice singing inspiring words about salvation and hope, or something inside him that was tired of tragedy, violence, and death, this particular trip seemed darker than ever. In fact, he felt as if both he and his truck were mere specks that could be swallowed up in darkness with the flicker of a fading star.

Bull's lips tightened just a bit, and he threw his huge shoulders back involuntarily, widened his eyes and exhaled loudly when he was asked to give Harold the news. He didn't answer right away. He turned and lumbered to the small storage area where the guards changed and sometimes slept. On the way, he took his coat off and then stopped to hang it in his locker.

He remained motionless for a minute, staring into the upper shelf as if he saw something that shouldn't be there, or something that gave answers to complex questions. He finally swung the locker door shut and reluctantly returned to where his colleagues awaited his response. He lowered his head as he approached and passed them, and nodded that he would do the dirty work of delivering the punch of another layer of bruising to the young inmate's heart.

A call was put in to get confirmation from the assistant warden on duty. Bull skipped his usual kick of black brew and downed a tall glass of water. Without a word, he left the checkpoint as the other guards watched with both relief and anticipation as Bull's huge form floated with incongruous silence through the still, dark hallway. His smooth stride belied the fact that he felt he was heading into and bringing more fire to the Connally boy's hell.

When Bull arrived, Harold appeared to be sleeping, still with the bloody gob of thin cloth covering most of his face. He looked a mess, Bull thought, and it crossed his mind just how much this latest news was going to help. He wished he had said no to being the bearer of the boy's latest nightmare. For some time, he just watched the young man at rest, perhaps even at peace. He almost turned back.

Harold's eyes opened. He sensed someone near him and heard both the breathing of someone large, and the muted clink of prison keys. The sound was akin to a Pavlovian signal. Each inmate had his own reaction, but they all had one. The jangle either meant food, a visitor or trouble — usually the latter. Harold didn't really care one way or another. He figured he was being checked again to see whether he was still bleeding. And he didn't care about that either.

"Hey, kid? Can I come in?" the big guard asked. He did so as softly as someone trained to yell and intimidate could.

Harold thought this strange, but he wasn't thinking straight, so perhaps he misheard, or maybe there was no one there at all. He didn't known what day it was and, sometimes, where he was, for hours at a time, even when he had been told.

"I'm comin' in, okay?"

Harold tried to turn his head. It was real, the voice and the presence, but he didn't understand why the guy was being so polite. What would he have done if Harold had said, "No, I'd prefer you didn't." The man with the keys was a giant. He could do whatever he wanted.

Bull looked around for somewhere to sit. There was no chair and he didn't want to sit on the kid's bed. He didn't want any misunderstandings or charges or anything like that. Plus, he couldn't stand to be too close to what he knew was going to be unimaginable human pain. He ended up sitting on the can. His behind, though hard and muscular from years of workouts, was big enough to spread right over the seat. It wasn't so uncomfortable that he took note.

Harold strained to watch him as the man looked around for seating and finally settled. He wished he could look into the man's face to ascertain what the hell was going on, but he knew that with any significant move, the bleeding would start up again in a rush. This wasn't a moment when he wanted to either be choking on it or preoccupied with controlling it.

Then, even in his more than foggy state, it hit him. He understood the reason for the visit. His transfer must be due. He was going to be hauled to another rough institution up state. After all, this was how it happened last time. They just came and got him in the dark, before the other inmates were up, and drove him to his next dungeon. He was concerned about how he'd dress himself. He'd bleed to death messily. He still had pressure between his eyes and a painful, pre-eruptive throbbing at the base of his nose, right through to the back of his head.

How was he going to move? There was only one guard this time and none of them were normally inclined to help an inmate get dressed. He felt exhausted, helpless and despairing at the thought of going through the process of getting up, showering and traveling, especially in the shape he was in.

Bull leaned forward and folded the huge fingers of his hands together, almost as if he were praying. His seemingly boneless elbows rested on his athlete's thighs. Meanwhile, Harold noted that this wasn't how it had been done last time. They had just clanged on his cell, told him to collect his things, chained him up and down, and pushed him into a dark, back hallway and eventually into a van. He couldn't understand this guy's manner. He looked and acted like an uncle dropping in for a beer and a talk, slow and easy-going, with a tinge of nervous sadness.

"Kid, something's happened."

Bull waited for Harold to ask what, but he didn't. He didn't even blink. His head was still turned slightly sideways so that he could see Bull if he wanted to, but he moved his eyes away, halfway to center where they had been positioned earlier.

Bull was finding this even harder than he had thought it would be. He wished the kid would make it easier for him by acting out, swearing at him, or being generally hostile, but the wish just made him feel worse. The kid looked pathetic, as if he were bleeding to death as a result of being in the fatal accident himself.

"It's your sister. She . . . ah . . . um . . . well, she had an accident last night."

Harold didn't move his eyes or his head, but if he was blinking before, he wasn't now. He looked like an animal waiting calmly to be shot and put out of his misery. His pulse quickened and was visible in his thin throat.

"She's . . . well, she didn't suffer much, they say, but she's, well, she's dead, kid."

Harold's eyes did nothing for a full two or three minutes. Then they slowly closed. Bull didn't move. He remained in the same position on the toilet seat, waiting, not knowing what to do. Finally, he broke the silence, more to get an indication of where the boy was at, than because he knew what to say, or felt comfortable saying anything at all.

"You okay? Can I, ah, I don't know, get you somethin'? I'm real sorry 'bout this, man. Really am. It's the shits."

When there was no response, Bull looked around the cell in silence, rubbing his hands together as if he were waiting for some kind of announcement or sign as to what to do next. After looking up and down and around the cell at least a dozen times, he suddenly focused on himself and on the fact that he was sitting on the toilet. He whispered some semi-profanity about how absurd he must look and rolled his eyes, but otherwise he didn't move. He couldn't — not yet. He didn't know when he'd feel he could.

By the time he did move, Bull was more than stiff. He ached and he had a round groove where the uncovered toilet bowl had burrowed into his posterior. Harold was still staring and the guard didn't know what else to say or do. He hoped they had located the chaplain by now, or maybe the prison physician. This kid was in real trouble. Even he knew Harold shouldn't be left alone to further digest the news.

"The chaplain'll be in pretty soon. We're lookin' for him. Soon as we get him here, he's yours, okay?" Bull felt as if he were telling the boy lunch would be in an hour and everything would be fine. He vowed never to agree to this kind of a task again. It was too damn painful. He could deal with locking men up and breaking up fights in the showers and cafeteria, but not with bringing more pain to the already broken heart of a depleted young boy.

"Then you can talk to him, or whatever you need to do. Okay?" He moved toward the bars. "You sure I can't, ah, get you something, or do you want me to stay here a while, or. . . ?" He didn't need higher education to tell that Harold was in another place — a place that he, as a reluctant prison guard, didn't know how to get to or to deal with, with any degree of effectiveness.

Harold's nose started to gush, and Bull was relieved to be able to do something concrete to help him. He told Harold where he was going before he went to fetch him another cloth. When he returned, Harold hadn't budged. However, the top one third of his cot was soaked with blood. When Harold didn't open his fist to take the cloth, Bull knelt down, gently removed the one held in Harold's grip and started to wipe the boy's face and neck with a fresh one. He studied his closed eyes and pale skin as he stroked they boy's head and face as if caring for and cleaning a small child.

Bull became frightened. He was unable to keep up with the gushing flow from Harold's insides and was convinced that the boy would likely lose conscious or worse without medical help. He uttered something that was supposed to be reassuring and left to implore someone to kick ass to get the physician in. Bull was not only scared, he was mad. For the first time in his adult life, in a situation with someone other than a member of his family, his vision blurred as he fought back moisture in his deep, dark eyes.

It was Bull's last duty of the day. He got permission and checked out, his first time ever. He was more than prepared to make the forty-five minute drive home so soon after he had come in. He'd use one of his valuable sick days, even a vacation day if he had to. He was useless now anyway, and he knew it. He'd had all he could take of blood and cages for this day.

He wondered about himself and the others who made a living there — especially when he forced himself to assume that he'd be alright tomorrow.

The chaplain was still nowhere to be found by late afternoon and the prison physician was reluctant to make an unscheduled visit to the prison to see a patient who was obviously just in shock and mourning. The doctor was clearly annoyed when the assistant warden called him and pressed him to come in.

Even after some coaxing, he still insensitively explained, patronizing the less educated prison official, by repeating that a kid with Harold's history was bound to take news like this badly. In fact, he said "killer kids" either feel nothing or a great deal, and this kid was just going through increased trauma and drama related to the damned mess he'd brought on himself and others. Doc, as the inmates and guards called him, told the A.W. to just leave him alone for a day, and then, if anything, to start to be a bit firmer about getting him back into a routine – nosebleed or no nosebleed, and regardless of this unfortunate latest development.

The A.W. was fine with the recommendation. He and the warden wanted Harold deemed fit for transfer when they got the word. They didn't want to be accused of messing up the process due to this latest screw up or complication in their assignment.

"When Harold calms down," Doc said, "so will the bleeding. It's due to drawn out anxiety attacks and the best thing to do is to get him up and focused. Why don't you all just back off and stop treating him as if he were a sick child for awhile? After all," he reminded the prison official, "the young man is a bloody murderer. He isn't in there to receive stroking or surrogate parenting!"

The assistant warden couldn't have agreed more, and said so, after asking for and being promised the doctor's assessment and prescription in writing.

A week later, during his regular clinic hours at the prison, the physician packed Harold's nostrils with cotton batten again and gave him some to put in periodically himself. He also gave him a coagulant to thicken his blood, something to lower his blood pressure, and a mild sedative.

He told Harold that the bleeding would stop when he got a hold of himself, when he accepted the consequences of his actions. Meanwhile, he told him, he should get back to his work in the prison, take on a new task, even look into some trade training, like fixing radios or plumbing, something he could put to use in prison environments for the rest of his life.

Harold hadn't said a word through the entire examination. He only moved when Doc called, "Next!" to reluctantly call in the next complainant.

Within about ten days, Harold spoke. During that week, he had received at least four calls from Dr. Rosenthal. She had obviously heard what had happened to Jessica and was trying, determinedly, to contact him. Rules or no rules, professional relationship or no professional relationship, this was serious. Spencer had called too, for legal reasons, but Harold wasn't available to speak to either of them.

Soon, Harold had spoken sufficiently in and around his cell to be transferred from the kitchen to crafts and carpentry. He was still bleeding on and off and he brought the fact that he might bleed into the food to the cook's and then the assistant warden's attention. He was reassigned within an hour.

Usually a change of duties takes weeks and, even then, if someone has something against you, you don't get it. It was well known, however, that most of the inmates were almost phobic about blood, especially that of others. They were all paranoid about getting AIDS, even though over two-thirds of the population was already HIV positive.

They came to refer to Harold's bleeding as his "nasal curse" and told him to wear a rag like any *real* lady would under the circumstances. Seemingly oblivious, Harold just walked around with wads of Kleenex and gauze sticking out of his nostrils. He'd twist and suck on pieces and then push them as far into his nasal passages as possible. A good bit was always left sticking out, so he looked as if he had snow-white and then, as the day went on, bloodied growths protruding from inside his head.

Whether it was due to the intrusion of Kleenex into his frontal lobe or something else, there developed a change in Harold's behavior. He seemed to be getting better, or as close to better as he could, given where he was and all that was lost to him.

He also appeared to be doing relatively well with the recently communicated fact that the new, official extension of his stay at this facility wouldn't last forever — there'd be a new facility, new guards and new hardened men to position himself with all over again. And he wouldn't know when this move and process would start. It would, as was the way, happen suddenly. He knew by now that there was no point in speculating, let alone in trying to exert control over his life circumstances

In crafts, he wanted to work with an old man the inmates came to call the "Whisperer," after some fellow in a book that many of them had been given by relatives, but few had actually read. They gave the aged man, imprisoned now for about thirty years, the new name because of his virtual silence, and the miraculous work he did with leather, including making and selling high-quality saddles on the outside. They used to call the man the "Marlboro Man" because he was tall, looked like he was an ancient, tired leftover from the wild west, and smoked constantly, even in the shower. He sometimes fell asleep at his work table with a butt hanging from the side of his dried lips.

He had a statewide reputation for his goods, but he was as modest and unassuming as a good priest. When he did speak, which was seldom, he literally spoke in a whisper, a result of having had his throat half-slashed in his early thirties in a fight about his being a half-breed, as the story went. As the name got around, he never whispered any opposition.

The Whisperer was a great guy to know and would be even better to work with, and Harold had observed him for a while and decided that he wanted to be with him. The man made custom leather jackets and pants as well, and all kinds of items for the guards and their families.

As a result, he had more privileges than anyone in the place. He even got more freedom and perks than the guy who did the electrical work for the warden. This other guy had set up a great stereo system in the warden's office and rewired his whole house, but he was younger, tougher and still had a restive taste for the outside.

The Whisperer was as content as a fish in calm, insect-filled waters. He wouldn't have left the place if they paid him to live on the outside. He was able to do what he loved, got all the supplies he needed free, and could pretty well do what he wanted when he wasn't running his own little cottage industry. Though his dwelling had bars, he didn't even reside under lock and key.

While observing, Harold had found the man intriguing, but had stayed out of his way, the way he did with all the inmates. During his period of silence, and following Jessica's death, he was thinking of him more and more. By focusing on getting the chance to work with him, and watching the man's rhythms, Harold reduced the number of times in an hour he lived and relived going through the windshield with, or instead of, Jessica.

He decided he'd somehow get to work with the man. He remembered once seeing all the leather, dye, strips and patches of different colors of worn pieces that one would then see later in an amazing jacket or vest. The old man worked out of a double cell that he had been provided with for his work. It was like a studio with a messy bachelor pad on one side. He was as busy as he wanted to be with huge, lucrative orders to fill at Christmas.

He also did custom birthday gifts for inmates' relatives, but the guards came first. They were the keepers who kept him free, living and working as if he were on the outside, but without the hassles and the pain of real life. He even decided when and if he locked his cell at night or at mealtime. He treasured his materials and his creations more than anything — and they were his ticket to the degree of freedom with which he was content. He coveted his productively protective nest as most people did their lives or loved ones. He was a true creator, wise and focused in the darkness of maximum security.

Harold liked that the Whisperer wasn't always looking over his shoulder. He didn't have to. He'd just go about his craft, minding his own business, and only speak if someone wanted something or if he was fitting someone for a vest, jacket, boots or whatever the order entailed. Harold was glad the elderly man didn't seem miffed when he did finally get permission to work and spend time with him. He just wanted to watch and learn. There was no telling what he might be able to do if he were given a chance.

The fact that Harold was still very quiet, both by nature and by circumstance, suited the Whisperer just fine. The man hummed a lot, but talking, especially chitchat, wasn't his thing. If someone was willing to do the dirty work — clean up, gather strips of leather and put them away by color, and deal with a "customer" while he worked, it was a perfect partnership.

With the double cell, two chairs and open bars which allowed one to take a short walk to stretch one's legs, it made for a prime assignment. Plus, the space was perfect for two quiet men. Harold didn't even mind the teasing about how they looked together. A few inmates came to calling them "Grandpa Walton and John-Boy" once they saw how well they worked together and how easily they communicated.

They were a sight to behold. The old man looked about 160 and, after his historic loss of blood and instinctive fasting, Harold looked from afar like a skinny, pubescent schoolboy. Only up close, where Harold didn't allow anyone to get, if he could help it, could one see in the boy obvious signs of premature aging and an edged air of resignation.

Harold had learned to smoke early in his prison stay, so the smoke the two generated was just fine for both of them, if initially blinding to a visitor. However, when his mentor in leather works wasn't smoking, he sucked and chewed tobacco with the noisy vigor of a starving wolf.

Further, when he deemed a chunk flavorless, he simply spat it in any convenient direction — anywhere where he wouldn't soil a product of his labor. Often, Harold was the inadvertent target of sputum soaked, brown gob. When he wasn't, he took it upon himself to clean it up before it stuck to the walls or the floor.

His first two days, he spent at least five hours scraping the stuff off the walls and the floor of the cell. The old man even had some crusted in and around his bed. The gathering mounds of tobacco pies didn't bother the man at all, but he didn't seem to mind that Harold cleaned them up either.

The only thing Harold wasn't sure of, was whether the quiet man took some pleasure in pulverizing him in the leg or butt with the stuff. He could spit it with the velocity of a well-made slingshot and it stung and stuck. Harold was almost sure that the first few times, when he had reacted with either shock or a muted gasp when he had taken a hit, that the Whisperer had grinned mischievously. The boy learned to remain alert and to dodge when under fire. Regardless, the spitfire invariably hit its intended or unintended target.

The prison officials were pleased to receive confirmation of Harold's allocution. Spencer had left a message for Harold to change one paragraph of what he had first written, and he had done so. In fact, the request had come indirectly via a guard when Harold wouldn't take calls after Jessica's death.

He had rewritten and finished it off while taking some hash given to him by an older inmate. He couldn't have done it if he hadn't been stoned. He couldn't have, again, gone through the details the judge demanded he submit. He would have started drowning in his own blood again, and whatever plans he had had for a change, or a strategy for prison life, would have gone out the window.

The "done deal" required one addition and rendition that Harold had to address and get over with. He was working on pulling himself together for a reason, a purpose, and he couldn't have what he saw as a judge's sick need for a gorier rendition of a nightmare throw him off course.

So, he managed to capture the reality of it all by writing about it in an altered state. He had thought it odd that he could be so obediently precise from a place of blurred sentiments and diminished capacity. He wished he had learned this earlier. He might have been able to bear living.

He still hadn't responded to Dr. Rosenthal's almost incessant calls. One message said that she would be coming back to visit, but he forced himself to phone her late one afternoon when he could both get to the phone, and when he suspected she would have left her office.

He left a message on her answering machine that he had a prison against prison softball game the day she suggested she visit, and wouldn't be able to see her. He said he'd let her know when he was free. He knew this would please her. She would be pleased that he was forming relationships and becoming involved in prison activities — almost as if he were at college, finally bonding and participating in healthy charac-

ter-building activities. It obviously worked. The calls stopped.
She was waiting comfortably, he suspected, for him to fit her
into his social calendar. He, too, felt clear about the way he
was adjusting and why. He knew he couldn't have pulled himself out of a state of bloody paralysis without having faced hard
facts and become both purposeful and decisive about the rest
of his life.

Because Harold was fifteen, and technically a minor imprisoned all along as an adult, the prison had to provide perfunctory reports on his progress and status, especially now that
his stay at the county prison had suddenly been extended by
the state due to over-crowding up north. They under-played
his bleeding spell and virtual muteness while over-playing his
cooperation and productivity with his new co-worker. They
used terms like "turned himself around," "recovering nicely
after the death of his sister," and "has become cooperative and
interested in working in crafts."

Social services were also delighted, though discreet. They
were ambivalent as to whether more should be done for the
boy, but they also kept secret any positive information, especially from the public. They didn't want to give the impres-
sion that the "killer kid" was happy or thriving.

The public needed to think that he was, as he had been,
crouched in the corner of a filthy cell bleeding to death. Solid
members of the community routinely asked each other if the
little bastard had yet been stabbed to death. Invariably, the
question initiated gleefully obscene discussions about the ways
and degrees in which and to which Harold must be suffering.
Most people needed to believe that he was enduring horrific
and highly imaginative forms of agony, concurrent with their
now nervous, defensive and angry approach to their own poisoned lives.

They'd be pleased, in a way, that he'd lost his sister, as an
added punishment of sorts. But they'd also hate him more for

causing her death. Either way, there was always new fuel, real or imaginary, to maintain the pleasing toxicity of well-stoked vengeance.

Harold knew what people were thinking. He had always been aware, if not able to define people's need to punish others for whatever reason, and to deflect ugliness from themselves. Whether it was Spencer, Rosenthal, the prison officials, or social services, he was glad they were all comfortable with their mandatory or discretionary roles regarding his actions and apparent progress.

Due to the apparent relief among and distraction of those who didn't want to know him, but had a stake in his condition, Harold rediscovered his safe, predominating inner world. He didn't think he was smart, but he was convinced that there could be no people on Earth as dumb as those celebrating his new posture and apparent attitude toward maximum security living.

He just hoped there was at least one person who had listened, among all those who didn't and don't, to how and where he had asked that Jessica be buried. Well after her death, with urgent sincerity, he requested that she be moved from a perfunctory burial spot to be buried by her parents in the same beautiful spot she had chosen for them. The Andersons had backed off in horror, depleted, when she died, allowing the city and an estate attorney to make the decision. He hadn't been consulted. Now, the request was all he ever wanted or needed them to hear.

It was pouring rain and forked lightening shot down from the skies, potentially decimating the land and any life it hit, as if in murderous scorn of those who take life for granted. The thunder was powerful enough to shake the 200-year-old structure as if it were made of plywood. The storm continued for hours and into the second hour, the electricity failed, and generators were turned on to illuminate the checkpoints, providing much duller, virtually useless lights in the wide hall-ways along the cell blocks.

The Whisperer took no heed. It might as well have been a sunny day in April for all he cared. He had his special issue candles, a lantern, and a massive, battery operated spotlight given to him a year ago by a guard in exchange for an intri-cately initialed leather vest.

He worked away diligently, smoking, chewing his wad of tobacco, humming his indecipherable melodies, totally oblivi-ous to the restive anger among inmates assuming they'd be disallowed their exercise time in the prison yard if the storm persisted. A simple man, he saw no irony in the fact that prison officials wanted to ensure that no one was naturally electro-cuted.

He also, as early morning began to emerge, didn't stop to notice that Harold hadn't joined him. They always started up well before the normal daily work hours, usually even before the breakfast call, but Harold hadn't slipped in, in his befit-tingly silent way. His young helper had learned to be so unob-trusive that he could arrive, leave for a pee, or for the day, and the man never even noticed. Into the third and fourth hour, however, when the old man would look over his shoulder ex-pecting to see the boy nearby, he started to wonder.

Harold had always asked him, using as few words as pos-sible, if something else was required of him, and he seemed to like being in the shop with the old man as early as possible. A man who long ago stopped wondering about anything, he ac-tually stopped stitching at one point and lifted his head to ponder Harold's whereabouts.

He wondered if Harold thought he had to stay in his cell, if he had misunderstood the announcement about there being no external movement during the storm. He wondered if the kid was stupid enough to think this meant that he couldn't come to join him. He shook his head, thinking this was prob-ably what happened, and went back to work.

An hour later, with the normal clatter and echoes going on above and beyond his cell, the old man wondered again. More irritated by the fact that he had come to enjoy, almost need, the boy's company, he uncharacteristically put down his work, locked his cell and went to the distant block to tell the kid to get his ass over to his shop. He'd make it look and sound official, as if he had been asked to fetch him, not that he had grown used to Harold's assistance and easy company.

The Whisperer liked the boy and he wasn't one to judge. He had seen enough in his life to know that one never knows about another human being. All he knew was that bad people do bad things and good things, and that the same goes for the so-called good folk. They were all the same except for degrees and crimes committed.

He knew there were millions of people pretending to be good citizens who had hurt more people, more deeply and irrevocably than half the inmates in his prison home. Of course, he didn't discuss this kind of thing. He didn't think his opinions, ideas or certainties held any weight under a fickle sun, nor did he care. He lived freely in a settled world of his creation, and he protected it by needing as little as possible, especially anything resembling the approval of others.

He reached Harold's relatively secluded cell after peering into a few others already vacated by their inhabitants for breakfast and duties. He *thought* he reached it, anyway. He wasn't sure. He had never been to Harold's cell, or any other for over ten years, and he felt strange this far from his own space. It was so dark with the still, dim light coming from the generators that he couldn't be sure.

He gripped a bar, leaned and looked sideways toward what he thought must be Harold's bed and saw that he wasn't there. He checked the can and he wasn't taking a crap either. He must have been called down by the warden or something, he thought, even though it was unusual for Harold not to come and tell him first. Unconcerned, and anxious to get back to his materials, he turned to go back to his own block and level when, out of the corner of his good eye, he caught a long shadow at the upper left-hand corner of the dark, square enclosure.

He looked again, and squinted to see what it was, but it wasn't clear. Something heavy, lifeless, and seemingly formless was swinging ever-so-slightly from where it hung each time the thunder hit and the building shook. His body tensed and the old man straightened up and pushed as much of his face and head through the bars as possible.

He squinted harder, cupping his eyes with his hands as if they were high-tech binoculars that would both magnify the object and light the cell.

⊲⊳⊲⊳⊲⊳⊲⊳

The Whisperer's hands slowly dropped away from his face. His eyes had widened to their normal size and intensity, something they hadn't the need nor the inspiration to do for thirty years. He stood for a moment in steadied silence, before whispering something into the dark shadows.

He knew what it was and, given who he was, part of him felt he could accept it and need only offer a throaty farewell and move on. Surely, he had been in prison and in an insane world too long to experience the emotions attached to loss or gain as they relate to the heart. But his insides churned with contradictory feelings, renewed sentiments that, were he thinking rationally, he wouldn't remember ever feeling before.

In a kind of primordial panic, the old man began to pull and push on the bars to Harold's cell. He fought and wrenched his body between two bars and pushed harder, emitting half-calling, half-grunting sounds as he tried to jam himself toward the boy with frantic violence.

The guards heard strange, animal-like, wailing sounds echoing from the corner of the upper cell block and moved quickly, two of them at once, in the direction of the area. From fifty feet, as if on cue, they reached for their keys, preparing to unlock the door to the cell. They knew before they even got there what they'd see. The guards who had any prior involvement with Harold had felt, at least prior to his latest assignment, that it was only a matter of time before he internally dove over the edge.

They let the Whisperer go to him and, as if following through on a well-rehearsed drill, the guards cut Harold down as the old man held and raised the boy's body, releasing the pressure from his neck. Just as the lights flashed back on with a loud crack and jolt, and sundry machinery groaned to life again, Harold fell, unconscious or dead, into the Whisperer's arms.

Shocked and shaken, the guards watched the older prisoner put his ear to Harold's chest. They remained immobile while the old man placed his mouth and dry, thin lips over the boy's opened mouth. He started to blow rhythmically, steadily, trying to will, as well as nurture, him back to life.

At the same time, as he tried to pour life from his own lungs into the boy, the Whisperer used one age-spotted, slightly crooked hand to gently remove the familiar strands of strategically woven leather strands from Harold's red, rutted neck. The now bright, unforgiving lighting was almost too much to bear.

The guards merely looked on with unusual empathy while they gave the Whisperer his shot at bringing the boy back. When they heard barely audible wheezing and choking sounds coming from somewhere between the boy and the man, and before they could react or ascertain who had made the sound, the Whisperer lifted and moved the boy out of the cell like an emergency physician with a patient in code blue.

The guards followed as the old man half-walked and half-ran, holding and carrying Harold as if he were as precious and as light as a small child. As the hustling group of men reached the next level down, and then the next, shadowed faces watched from behind bars in squinting silence, and with a kind of fearful, sad respect.

For hardened, seemingly unthinking men, they knew much about resignation and letting go. They all resisted it, kept it at bay like the devil itself. They instinctively knew what Harold had done, and the fact that the Whisperer was involved, seeing him venturing into the belly of the prison with the boy's flaccid body in his arms, made the procession almost sacred.

The prison had never been so quiet. Except for the clattering of briskly moving prison-issue boots and curt calls ahead to open doors to sections of the prison on the path to the infirmary, there was dead silence.

The old man wouldn't let go of Harold's body when they reached the clinic. The nurse on staff tried to coax him to unwrap his arms from around the still limp and blue-white skinned, unmoving form. She signaled to the guards to help her and they took the man gently by the shoulders to pull him away.

The Whisperer muttered something in what sounded like a foreign language as he moved back from the boy and stopped two yards away in a corner to watch and wait, making sure that his gaze did not leave the young inmate's deathly, expressionless face. The guards and the nurse tacitly agreed to allow him to stay as Harold was given oxygen, repeatedly called to by name, and gently slapped on either side of his face.

They waited, the guards in silence, the nurse ready to do more when and if there was a change in Harold's still semi-comatose state. The Whisperer sat propped in a corner, muttering a prayer or chant, old words accessed to heal and call to the depths of a tattered, young soul.

The prison physician arrived and noted that while

Harold's heart was beating weakly, his breathing was extremely labored. There was no telling when and if he would fully emerge to consciousness.

Moreover, no one knew how long he had been hanging there, and what would be left of him if he did return. The physician did know that Harold needed hospitalization, however, and arranged for an ambulance. The thin strands of tough, treated leather had gouged the front of the boy's neck and injured both his windpipe and his esophagus. It might even have cut into his trachea. If so, whether he lived or died, was brain damaged or not, he wouldn't be saying much, at least not much that could be understood.

After attaching two intravenous bags of clear fluids and giving him an injection to support and increase the timid beating of his heart, paramedics wheeled Harold's body out of the small cubicle. The guards helped with doors and stairs as the Whisperer sat, as still as a statue, in the place where he watched the paramedics administer to what was left of Harold's life. By the time the guards returned, however, he had disappeared.

The elderly man had returned to Harold's barren cell, and was sitting against one wall, running the strands of blood-soaked leather through and around his fingers and hands, over and over, as if he could both wipe them clean and return them, untouched and unused, to his private stash.

It must have taken some time, he thought. The boy had assiduously gathered each strand, day to day adding to the thickness and strength of a deadly cord. He wondered how the boy got it past him — the bits and pieces of leather, and the entire process, the strategy. How had he allowed himself to become so comfortable with Harold, and so easily trusting, that he hadn't noticed any depletion in his supplies or un-usual lumps or creases in the boy's simple clothing?

Nothing was clear to the man, especially something in-tangible that he couldn't have put into words if his life depended on it. He was perplexed, in a way frightened, by where his heart, mind and gut, even his soul, had gone regarding the boy and what he had done to himself.

He felt overwhelmed, sodden with emotions. He was *feeling*, and it wasn't good. In spite of or because of their hours of silence together, he had come to care deeply for the boy. With these feelings had come other emotions that were new and confusing, as if he, too, were a young boy just learning the ropes regarding relationships, boundaries, and love. It hit him that, for the first time in decades, he had felt both joy and hope.

As he pensively returned to his open cell, he gripped the strands of damp leather in his right hand. He kept gripping what had encircled Harold's neck and choked him to near death, even as he fell asleep for an hour or so and woke again. He only loosened his grip when he got word of his silent partner's condition. The boy had survived, and if he wanted to, he would also live to talk about it.

FOURTEEN

New Beginnings

T HE WHISPERER APPEARED TO RETURN to his old routine within hours of hearing about Harold's initial recovery and subsequent, temporary placement in a psychiatric facility. If there was any change in the older man, it was that he seemed quieter than ever and less patient with the various guards' descriptions of customized orders for themselves, and their wordy attempts to describe the particulars of items for their spouses or offspring. His endurance for small talk, or for talk of any kind, had been eroded to virtually nil.

Once seemingly sanguine and unaffected by normal human moods, the old man now seemed even more reclusive and more easily irritated by the mere presence of others, let alone by actual visits. Even the chaplain, having heard about his manner and mood, decided to stay away. If anyone could work through his inner turmoil, this wise man could. Moreover, Ben felt confident in thinking he knew what was bothering the man and to what extent he had been changed.

When Harold returned to the prison three months later,

he didn't lower his head upon entry. Nor did he skulk as he was escorted to a cell three down from where he had attempted to commit suicide. He took the same route through which he had been frantically carried in the Whisperer's arms months before, and he walked it like a young man, who was now at least working on fathoming or discovering his worth.

When he got to his new cell, he half-turned to thank his escorting guards — new fellows who were a little wary of their ward, given his history — and arranged the few belongings he had there. He looked more like a traveler shuffling things around at a room at the "Y" than he did a boy trying to improve the aesthetics of a prison cell. To an observer, he might have appeared to be glad to be back.

Harold was given a choice and went back on kitchen duty while he figured out how to approach his former, informal boss and co-worker. He knew what the Whisperer had done, having been told and having discussed it in sessions at the hospital, and was curious to see the man again. He also needed to apologize.

He had not only stolen from a man who evidently cared for him; he had used the man's hard begotten wares to design a way to attempt to kill himself. Now that he knew what the quiet, old man had done for him, talking to him felt impossible, but necessary. Harold felt both ashamed and guilty, yet grateful that the Whisperer had shown such concern and been so intent upon saving him. No one had ever tried before and no one, as far as he could remember, had ever carried him to any kind of safety.

Harold continued to express his awe at the Whisperer's actions in bi-weekly sessions held at the prison and begun at the hospital. Soon, he would be transferring to an institution for serious juvenile offenders and doing even more therapy while taking courses to complete high school. Harold knew that somehow approaching the man had to happen soon. He couldn't just leave — not without both saying goodbye and looking into the eyes of someone who, for no particular reason, thought he had been worth the price the old man paid for showing his feelings for him. Ironically, one result of trying to die, and almost succeeding, was that Harold had found some small wonders in living.

A week before he was to be transferred, Harold asked permission to go to the man's cell and work area before embarking on his duties in the kitchen. The administration had been informed by what was now Harold's caseworker, as well as by a panel of supervising psychiatrists, that this should be a mandatory part of his last experience in the large, adult prison. Permission was granted and the timing was left up to Harold.

The man's back was to him the way it always had been when Harold arrived in the mornings. Harold had planned his morning arrival so that it would be identical in both time and manner to the hour and way he had joined the man in prior months.

Harold knew that the old man was aware of both his entering his space and his standing about five feet behind him. He stood in silence, fascinated by the familiarity of the old man's rounded back and quick, efficient hands and arms. *Just like old times*, Harold noted. And just like old times, he knew that he would have to be the first to talk.

Harold still paused, wondering how things could seem so familiar — as if nothing had happened to interrupt the quiet cadence of their synchronicity. Yet, so much had happened. For one thing, he wasn't visiting under any pretense and with any ulterior motive. The man had displayed his bond with the boy for the entire prison to see.

Finally, Harold hummed a hello in the direction of the man's slightly tightened back, receiving a nod in return. Harold wondered if his friend was angry. Perhaps he had become indifferent. After all, it had been a while since Harold had scared

him to near death, or, reluctantly for the Whisperer, to life.
While he understood why the Whisperer had not been to see
him once he knew he was back, at the same time, he had to
wonder if coming to see him was the right thing to do.

At the very least, Harold felt a fascination. He wanted to
look into his eyes — eroded, caring eyes he remembered seeing repeatedly while both regaining consciousness in the hospital and in subsequent dreams and sessions.

"I'm sorry," Harold said timidly, almost inaudibly. The
man just nodded again.

"I mean, I'm sorry I stole your stuff and . . . used it the way
I did. I really didn't mean to involve you. I promise." Harold's
feet stayed in place, but his body leaned forward and his neck
strained to see the man's profile. Just as he was straining to
focus on one side of the mouth that had forced life into his
body, the man turned slowly on his old, worn stool.

"You did," the old man whispered, appearing to focus on
the leatherwork in his hands. "You did mean to involve me.
You stole from me to kill yourself, and you knew I would come
looking. You knew."

Harold's face reddened and he looked away, perplexed.
He hadn't been aware of making the assumption that the man
would come, but it didn't feel wrong or inaccurate either.

"How do you know?" Harold whispered in earnest, ready
to accept the man's explanation.

"Just know," the Whisperer responded. He looked up. "I
know by the way you took my air, and by the way you moaned
when I carried you. You knew. But I think you needed proof."

Harold looked down at the floor, at his own sneakers,
and then at the bare feet of his mentor, friend and savior.
"Maybe," he uttered quietly. "Maybe you're right."

The man nodded the same way he would have nodded in
the old days if Harold had asked him if he wanted another cup
of coffee.

"I want to. . . well, I want to say thanks," the boy said, moving closer. He stopped when he felt the man tense and recoil somewhere inside, as if he were now afraid of Harold's coming close.

"Are you staying?" the Whisperer suddenly asked.

Harold was perplexed by the question. He assumed that the man knew that he was now being transferred to a better place to receive treatment, attend classes and, eventually, years and years away, a parole if he got better and worked really hard toward it.

"Staying? I thought y—"

"Are you staying with us, under this moon and stars, on earth?" the man clarified, as if irritated.

Harold was taken aback by the man's uncharacteristic interruption, and by his suddenly growing very serious and pale. No one had or would ask this question so bluntly and clearly. "I . . . I . . . think so. I'm trying," he answered pensively with an undefined eruption of pain. "I'm sure gonna try."

"Good," the old man said, as he slid back into a position with his back to Harold. "You should. And you've gotta make it. You have things to do."

"Like you," Harold responded with apparent enthusiasm, looking around at the man's accumulated work.

"No," the man looked down with softened, tired eyes. "Not like me. Like you, boy. Like *you*." He turned his head ever so slightly in the boy's direction. "You have your own work to do, your own creations, and they are of the mind and heart. You'll learn how to make and use them."

Harold was confused, but he wasn't about to argue. He had just wanted a chance to connect with this man who had first accepted him, and then risked emerging into the world to save him. Harold noticed the taciturn lowering of the man's head and eyes.

The old man seemed reluctant to look at him or to face

him, as if he were embarrassed, and as if it was he who had almost died and come back to life, saved by the boy, not the other way around.

"I like you, too, y' know," Harold deliberately mumbled, showing no indication of how surprised he was by what he had blurted out.

The Whisperer nodded. He knew that Harold had felt safe and useful with him, but he had to wonder if Harold knew what he had both given and taken from him. He knew he couldn't explain.

As if in understanding, Harold slowly approached the man from behind and put his hand on his shoulder. To his surprise, the Whisperer dropped the three strands in his left hand, paused to take in the minor mishap, and then, without turning around, raised his arm across his chest and placed his weathered palm and fingers over Harold's.

The old man's head and face were still turned away. It was difficult to tell who was comforting whom, or whether they were comforting each other. Harold did not see the bulbous tear run slowly and crookedly down one side of the man's yellowed cheek. Leaning forward in concentrated diligence, the man used every tired muscle in his body to signal the boy to leave. In fact, he knew he would never see Harold again. In silent understanding, Harold backed up slowly, paused, and then turned and re-entered the wider world of the prison.

Harold's transfer came through more quickly than anyone at the prison thought, and, within ten days, he was packing his meager belongings and preparing to be carted off by a van headed for the "Boy's Farm" — an appropriate euphemism for a boy's prison in which hard work, education, and intensive therapy were the principles that both defined and drove the institution.

The experience was new and different right from the time of the announcement. For one thing, Harold wasn't afraid to go. He had heard much about it from his now steady therapist, as well as in what had become regular and usually congratulatory letters from Dr. Rosenthal.

She had even asked to accompany him on the trip to the farm on her day off. After a few visits at the hospital when Harold had been intensely watched and bombarded with psychotherapy, they had become friends in a way. He was no longer angry with her, and she was no longer afraid of him or the consequences of becoming involved with him.

Dr. Rosenthal also grew to better understand how and in what kind of an emotional space Harold had been lost. She didn't doubt, however, that he had a long, hard road ahead of him, and that he would need all the understanding and support he could possibly come by, especially in the form of acceptance and friendship.

Although some of the community and nation at large would forever judge him harshly, with his newfound clarity, Harold's greatest enemy would continue to be himself. At least he would now live, eat, and bunk in closer to normal surroundings with other boys who had also lost track and perspective. He would learn to connect with others who shared his experience of a world that felt bereft of love and replete with criticism.

Further, he would have a chance to learn again with teachers — men and women who also knew and understood both *his* suffering and the suffering he had caused others. They were trained to tend to the effects of both sides of the ongoing, punitive grind at the core of Harold's heart and life.

Epilogue

THREE BOYS WAITED THEIR TURN as the assistant for Con's office tried to bring order to the desk, as well as to the general mess of files and forms leaning and piled against the walls of the waiting area. The strong smell of her perfume further crowded the small area.

They watched the pretty woman with the naive fascination of boys living with boys, forgetting the tough, raunchy talk shared in showers and the gym. The woman was supposedly Con's wife and they believed it because of her ease around them. She wasn't at all afraid. Even though they had been called to Con's office because they were in some kind of trouble, she treated them as if they were just teens in for a Pepsi and a burger. They liked her a lot, and it made waiting to see Con not only easy, but almost worth whatever their "work off" — the new facility's term for punishment — was going to be.

They had to look away periodically when the woman caught them staring and smiled. Luckily, there was much to pretend to look at other than the lady. Even though they had seen all the diplomas and other showcased papers hanging crookedly on the waiting room walls before — at interviews, at registration, and before other one-on-one meetings with the administrator — they could still lose themselves in the chunks of the mysterious story they hinted at.

There was an ancient newspaper clipping about a skinny kid killing some other kids and something about the police going to his home, and what looked like prison documents, noting transfers, furloughs, parole hearings, denials, and a final acceptance. Many diplomas — at least four, with fancy writing and stamped gold or bright red, round symbols in the bottom corners — were believed to be Con's.

Some of the boys had parents with lots of diplomas and degrees and they weren't at all like Con, but they allowed their kids to be put in his care. Even the boys didn't understand the way he did things, especially when they got in trouble. Con was serious, for sure, and you had to tow the line, but the boys always felt as if he understood them. He never, as one of the boys put it, "acted superior." And he never humiliated them or ignored their feelings or opinions.

The door to the inner office finally opened and another young man, a buddy of the waiting boys, emerged, obviously having taken some time to try to wipe away both tears and the open, pink, facial swelling that comes with them. The boys made supportive eye contact and then looked down with respect and empathy.

Then Con followed, removing his glasses and scratching his greying beard on the right side of his face, as if he were recovering in some way himself. He muttered something to the lady, and checked an appointment book on the cluttered desk. He looked tired, but he was old, in his late forties or maybe even older, so fatigue was normal, the boys thought, even though they knew they added to it by giving him grief.

They continued to wait with the renewed look of contrite culprits until the man straightened up, rubbed the back
of his neck and mildly, calmly, but with no mistaking his au-
thority, uttered the word, "Boys?"

They scrambled to a standing position and moved en
masse, bumping into each other in the tiny hallway to his office. The woman grinned warmly as she heard the otherwise
mischievous young men verbally saluting her husband as they
awkwardly entered his always busy, adolescent-filled office.

"Yes, Sir," one or two would say. "Yes, Mr. Connally," some
would say, trying to gain an edge by using his name.

Though they all called him "Con" out of his presence,
and when referring to him with outsiders, only his adult friends
and most of the staff actually referred to him directly by his
informal name. In fact, the kids didn't even know his real first
name, or if Con *was* his first name. It gave the boys another
reason for trying to read the script on the diplomas – if they
were, in fact, his. There was just no way his name could be
"Con Connally."

That's a jailhouse name, as they called it, a prison name.
No, he must have picked it up because of his work with prison
kids, with "kid criminals," even though he was cool enough,
especially for a psychologist, and understanding enough and
sufficiently fair, to carry it off, to own it in a strange way.

Regardless of how he got it, he was just Con and, for some
uncanny reason, most of the boys strived for his quiet respect.
They felt somehow more comfortable when they knew he was
in the facility rather than on the road giving speeches and
talking to kids, teachers, prison officials and parents in other
states and countries.

When he was there, at the institution — even if he was
tired from all his traveling — the place felt safer, more like
home. They knew with Con that, no matter what happened,
chances were they'd be heard, understood and eventually

known for who they were. This was the first step toward the most precious kind of healing and freedom.

And it was one of the things a boy-come-man had learned that he could create and give. He had learned the hard way, starting with himself.

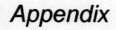

Appendix

Discussion Questions

CHAPTER ONE: Died Down

A. Harold has been asked by a psychologist to write about his life – and of the incident if he chooses.

1. How would you describe Harold's mood at this point?

2. What, if anything, are his current feelings about shooting his schoolmates?

3. How do you think that *you* would feel within hours or days of an involvement in such a trauma?

4. What, if anything, do you learn about his parents, or his feelings about them from what he has said so far?

5. Why do you think that Harold had difficulty for a couple of days remembering everything that happened from the shooting, to the arrest, and being taken to his cell?

6. Do you think that you would remember everything or forget for a while the way Harold did?

7. Why do you think that Harold did not feel the pain in his shoulder for a while?

8. Does Harold seem afraid? Why or why not? Would you be afraid? Why or why not?

9. What do you know so far about Harold's feelings toward himself?

10. Who, if anyone, does Harold consciously miss at this point?

11. How does it feel to answer these questions? Discuss your feelings with a parent, teacher, another adult, or a friend. Feelings are good – talking about them is even better. *Think about how you are feeling as you answer the questions in the rest of the book.*

CHAPTER TWO: Home Alone

1. If you were Harold's friend, would you think that he might have problems from some of the things he thinks and says? Give several examples.

2. As a parent of one of Harold's acquaintances, what would you do if you heard him speak the way he does on the tape for and to Dr. Rosenthal? What would you do, as an adolescent, if you heard him speak this way and knew he was sincere?

3. How does Harold feel about "feeling?" Generally, does he feel a great deal, very little or not at all? Explain. What, if he could have, should he have done with his feelings?

4. How would you, personally, describe how Harold might really feel inside? Give examples from what he says to support your opinion.

5. Did and does Harold "hate" his parents? Explain.

6. The irreversible nature of Harold's actions aside, do you think that Harold is a "monster?" Why or why not?

7. If you had met Harold a few years ago, in school, and he was annoying and rude, how would you have reacted to him? If you met someone like him now, would you react or treat him (or her) any differently?

8. As much as you can tell at this point, why is Harold so angry?

9. Do you think Harold is smart? Explain.

10. Why do you think Harold is so bitter about adults in general? Do you feel the same way, never the same way, or just sometimes the same way? Explain and discuss

11. Have you ever hurt an animal? If so, when? How did you feel?

CHAPTER THREE: Shades of Gray

1. Who do you think Harold feared most in his life?

2. Do you think he should have stayed at Hawthorne Academy? Why? Why not?

3. If you didn't know that Harold eventually killed his parents, would you consider him a violent person? Explain.

4. Is Harold angry? If so, again, what do you think he is most angry about?

5. Do you think Harold is below average, average or above average intelligence?

6. What, if anything, does Harold respect? If he does respect something or someone, why does he?

7. Why do you think it has become easy for him to talk into the micro-cassette recorder? Do you think it might be a good exercise for him in some way? Explain.

8. Why do you think Dr. Rosenthal has chosen this method (for the most part) to get him to talk? Under circumstances of your own, are there things you would find easier to talk about if you were alone, with a recorder? What might those things be?

9. What, if anything, do you have in common with Harold?

10. Why does Harold say he swears so much? Do you swear a lot? If so, why do you think you do?

11. Do you ever have violent thoughts? If so, when? Do they make you feel guilty? Discuss.

CHAPTER FOUR: Momentum

1. Why, from what you know so far, do you think Harold had headaches?

2. Is there anything you like about Harold? If so, what?

3. Given what we know about Harold so far, would you have befriended him? If not, why? If so, why?

4. Why do you think some teachers were a bit tough on Harold? Would he be an easy student to have in a class? Explain.

5. What do you think of Harold's opinions about teachers? Why do you think he is so angry with and hard on them? Do you share any of his feelings about teachers? Explain and discuss.

6. What do you think about Harold's thinking about what is real, isn't real, and what is made to seem real? Explain your thinking and feelings.

7. At this point in Harold's life, is he "lost?" If so, in your opinion, how and why? What, if anything, could someone have done to stop the momentum toward tragedy?

8. If Harold were your brother, would you be worried about him? Why or why not?

9. If Harold were a member of your student body, would you mock him, ignore him, treat him civilly or treat him in some other way? Explain.

10. Have you ever imagined doing violent things to people when you are angry with them? Do you think it is normal or abnormal to have these intense feelings sometimes?

CHAPTER FIVE: Out of the Sun

1. Do you think there was any particular reason that Harold did what he did on this specific day?

2. Do you think that Harold felt anything as he did what he did to his parents? Explain.

3. How did you feel when you read the section on Harold's killing his parents? Explain and discuss.

4. Why do you think Harold was able to continue to the schoolyard after killing his parents?

5. Have you ever thought of hurting or killing your parents? Why? How do you feel about having thought that way? Sick? Guilty? Scared? All of the above? Explain and discuss.

6. Have you ever thought about killing friends or fellow students? Why and when? If you have, what did you do with your feelings?

7. Do you think or remember from any part of the book so far whether or not Harold ever thought of committing suicide? If so, why do you think he might have wanted to take his life?

8. Why do you think Harold committed the ghastly act of killing the students at his school? Why did he ignore the young children outside?

9. Were Harold's motivations to kill his parents and the children the same, different or related? Explain.

10. Do you think Harold is brave, lost, crazy, lonely, cowardly, confused or...? Explain and discuss.

11. When you hear about these kinds of tragic incidents, how do you feel? Discuss.

CHAPTER SIX: Dead and Alive

1. Without using Harold's words, describe how he is handling the local prison.

2. Why would a lawyer be reluctant to represent Harold?

3. Why is Harold fixated on Dr. Rosenthal visiting him? What does she represent to him?

4. Is Harold glad about what he did? Explain.

5. Does anything Harold say make sense? If so, give examples.

6. What does Harold mean about parents or adults lying to kids?

7. Why do you think Harold feels relatively comfortable in prison? How did he explain it?

8. What do you think about his comments about being aware of and "respecting" other peoples' moods? Is this something that should be done out of prison? If so, why? Discuss.

9. Is Harold still angry? Explain.

10. Why do you think Harold is proud of not crying? Should he be? Explain.

CHAPTER SEVEN: Darkening Light

1. Why is Harold suddenly more fearful than before?

2. Why does Harold not want anyone to know the things he told Dr. Rosenthal on tape?

3. Why do you think Harold doesn't want to move on to another facility?

4. How would you feel about moving on if you were he? Explain.

5. Who does Harold trust at this point, if anyone? Discuss.

6. Would you feel "alone" in Harold's position?

7. Might your feelings build over time after committing the kind of violent act he committed? Explain and discuss.

8. How do you feel about Harold's remarks that no one cares about anyone else, especially about the "uncool" kids or those without boyfriends or girlfriends? Can you understand his feelings? Explain and discuss.

9. Do you think Harold is generally angry? If so, do you think he has been angry for some time? Even before the crime? Explain.

10. Have you ever felt like Harold? Trapped? Hopeless? Angry? If you have, share when you have felt this way. Discuss.

11. Who would you go to if you felt this way?

12. Do you feel fear for Harold at this point? If so, why?

13. Harold frequently uses so-called "bad" language. Why do you think this is? When you use bad language, why are you using it? To release frustration, anger, hurt...? Explain and discuss.

CHAPTER EIGHT: The Winding Road

1. Putting aside how the author described Harold's reactions, how do you think he felt the morning when he was awakened to be transferred? How would you feel?

2. Do you think that it is possible for Harold to be honest *and* to have killed people? Explain.

3. What do you think of the "abuse excuse" that Harold's lawyer might have been trying to set up for him?

4. Why, in your opinion, does Harold not just make something up to present to a judge in order to get sympathy? Why won't he cooperate?

5. Why do you think he still wants to see Dr. Rosenthal? Explain and discuss.

6. What do think is going to happen to Harold? At this point in his story, do you care? Why? Why not?

7. What does Harold mean by "it's crap?" What is he personally referring to about life by using the term repeatedly? Explain and discuss.

8. Do you think that there was a part of Harold that wanted and would have changed his life as it had been before he killed? Do you think he could have done so with the right help? Explain and discuss.

9. Do you think Harold is capable of loving someone? If so, why do you think he has been unable to form lasting, solid connections with others so far in his life?

10. At this point, do you like or dislike Harold? Why or why not? If you could write him a letter right now that would remain confidential, what would you say to or tell him?

11. As an exercise, write Harold a letter that you think would mean a lot to him and that says something about you and your feelings and life.

12. Have you found any part of this book frightening? If so, explain.

CHAPTER NINE: Waiting Alert

1. Name at least three specific aspects of prison that Harold fears.

2. What motivated Harold to try to learn the prison "culture" as quickly as possible? Was it conscious, unconscious or both?

3. Do you see Harold as brave, pragmatic or both?

4. What are the main feelings that Harold is dealing with in the new prison? Explain.

5. How would you feel in this prison? Explain and discuss.

6. What does Harold mean by becoming someone's "girl-friend?"

7. Realistically, who can Harold reach out to for support?

8. What would you do (*even though you wouldn't commit the ghastly crime Harold committed*) if you were in Harold's shoes? Would there be someone you could reach out to?

9. In what way is Harold "tricking" himself regarding the possibility of being placed elsewhere? Does he know he's doing this? Have you ever done this?

10. If you were in such a prison, would you obey? rebel? give up? fight? react some other way? Explain.

11. Do you think Harold should be tried as an adult with adult consequences to his act? Explain.

CHAPTER TEN: Dread Talking

1. Would you say that Harold is highly intuitive? Why or why not?

2. Why did Harold stop the tape for awhile when the subject of his sister came up? Explain and discuss.

3. Would Harold want Dr. Rosenthal to see him in his new cell? Why? Why not?

4. If he is smart, why did all this happen, initiated by him? Explain and discuss.

5. Do you think Harold is "insane?" Why? Why not? Explain and discuss.

6. What does Dr. Rosenthal mean when she talks about how the "tabloid approach" has made this and other tragedies worse? Explain and discuss.

7. Give at least one *intangible* reason for why the community hates him to the point of wanting him dead?

8. Do you think vengeance is a common emotion? Do you think it is positive or negative? When have you ever felt vengeful? Explain.

9. Does Harold feel very close to Dr. Rosenthal or is there another, more complex reason for his reaching out to her? Would you reach out under the same circumstances?

10. What would you do regarding Harold if you were Dr. Rosenthal?

11. When you feel lonely, "unknown" and misunderstood, what do you do? Would you do anything differently now after reading about Harold? Explain and discuss.

12. Who, in your life, understands you the most (*excluding pets!*)?

CHAPTER ELEVEN: Sister Fact

1. What had Dr. Rosenthal represented to Harold and what did she become to him by the time of this last meeting?

2. Had Harold totally given up caring about his defense? Explain.

3. Do you think that Harold was able to hurt Dr. Rosenthal emotionally? Is this how he really wanted to be? Explain.

4. Do you think that, given the state he was in, he could have hurt Dr. Rosenthal physically? Explain why or why not.

5. Why did Mr. Spencer, the lawyer, seem to do as little as possible for Harold and his case?

6. If you were a lawyer, would you want to defend Harold? Why? Why not? Does he deserve a proper defense after what he did?

7. Do you think it fair and appropriate that Harold was given no opportunity for regular counseling after his arrest?

8. Was Dr. Rosenthal afraid of Harold, just confused by him, or both? Explain.

9. Were all the professionals and officials a little "frightened" by Harold? Why or why not?

10. Do you think that part of the reason Harold yelled was to end the session by being forced to? If so, why would he need or want to do so?

11. In addition to bruises and scratches, what else was Dr. Rosenthal seeing when she thought Harold looked old?

12. Did Harold's sister's letter induce a drastic shift in Harold's "head space" and attitude? If so, why?

CHAPTER TWELVE: Done Deals Done

1. Why was Harold so resistant, even rude to Dr. Rosenthal?

2. Why do you think Harold looked "old?"

3. Did Dr. Rosenthal handle Harold well? What might she have done or said differently?

4. What, in your opinion, did Jessica come for? What did she need from Harold in order to go on?

5. Why do you think Harold "acted out" for a while, as in getting into fights, before the visit?

6. If you had done what Harold had done, would you find it difficult to write an allocution?

7. Why or how do you think Harold can have killed his parents and still long for them, especially for his mother?

8. Explain Harold's feelings about "redemption." In a general sense, what does it mean and why does he resist it?

9. Explain why Harold was terrified to see his sister.

10. Explain (don't describe) what happened during the meeting with his sister. What was going on with each of them? Why do you think Harold virtually collapsed at the end of the visit? Discuss.

CHAPTER THIRTEEN: Manageable Outcomes

1. Had Harold thought things out before he shot his parents and other school children? Do you think other children who kill think about the consequences of their actions before the fact? Explain and discuss.

2. Why did Harold, at one point, seem settled in prison? Explain.

3. Why do you think Harold came to have such a violent nosebleed after his sister's visit?

4. Related to the previous question, what do you think happened in his "inner world" prior to, during and after his sister's visit?

5. Why do you think Harold wouldn't take Dr. Rosenthal's calls after Jessica's death?

6. Do you think Harold liked the Whisperer? Explain and discuss.

7. Let's assume Harold liked the quiet man who worked with leather. Was he also using him? If so, in what way(s)?

8. Do you think, in his quiet way, the Whisperer liked Harold? Why or why not? Explain and discuss.

CHAPTER FOURTEEN: New Beginnings

1. How do you feel about Harold after reading this book?

2. Do you think that the author is sympathetic to Harold? Why or why not? Does he deserve any sympathy?

3. We know Harold killed children as well as his parents and that it is a tragedy, a terrible waste and more. But do you think that what happened to Harold was a waste too? Explain why or why not.

4. Who was there, throughout, for Harold to turn to in his loneliness – before and after the shootings?

5. If you knew someone like Harold, someone who was a loner, awkward, unpopular and a little eccentric, how would you treat him or her now? Why?

6. Have you ever felt as alone as Harold obviously felt before the shootings? Have you ever felt as alone as he clearly felt after the shootings? When, and what did you do about it? Would you do anything different now?

7. Who would you go to if you felt frightened, depressed, lonely or "invisible" at this point in your life?

8. Harold felt no one cared about him, or knew him – and that may have been what pushed him over an emotional edge into a life sentence. If you felt this way, what would you do?

9. Name three people who care that you are alive and would want to know if you had problems or were hurt? Who loves *you*?

10. Do you feel that your school provides someone who could help you if you became "lost" or despairing? Why or why not? If not, what would you suggest be set up in your school to help students deal with their feelings when they become overwhelming or before?

11. What affected you the most about this book? Explain.

12. Would you give this book to a friend in a serious emotional state, or ask a teacher or parent first? Why should you consult a teacher or another adult first?

13. Do you think it is a good idea to try to understand children and teenagers who kill? Do you feel you understand Harold? If so, explain him to an imaginary person with whom you are having an imaginary discussion.

14. Have you learned anything about your own feelings as a result of reading his story? If so, what?

About the Author

Dr. Lauren Woodhouse was born in Montreal and has studied in both Canada and the United States. Among other contributions, she is an author, essayist, broadcaster, psychotherapist, Victim-Witness Counselor, Trauma Specialist, and teacher. She is also on the International speaking circuit as an educator-entertainer, presenting both entertaining and serious "facts and fixes" related to the human condition in the new millennium.

Long involved in forensic psychology, the author works with troubled youth and earned, as one of her undergraduate degrees, a Bachelor of Education from Queens University in Ontario, Canada. She both taught and counseled young and older teens before she left teaching to focus on counseling, criminology, performance psychology and psychotherapy. She counsels inmates in medium and maximum-security penitentiaries and does ongoing consulting work for penitentiaries' services and programs.

At the Southern California University for Professional Studies, where she earned her Doctorate in Psychology, she did groundbreaking research on teen violence, particularly as it manifests in gangs. The author continues to work in Crisis Intervention, Debriefing, and Domestic Violence Intervention, and is frequently called upon to do television analysis related to child and adolescent violence.

Dr. Woodhouse is a member of the Canadian Psychological Association, the American Psychological Association and the Canadian Mental Health Association. She is also the founder of The International Institute for Child Security, an international organization comprised of social scientists, psychologists, physicians, teachers, parents and adolescents dedicated to addressing adolescent and child violence and suicide.

Other publications by Dr. Woodhouse include:

Laughing in the face of Change - *A Blueprint for a Return to Joy!*

Essential Adjustments- *Showing Up for Life in the New Millennium*

By Way of Sanity - *13 Principals for Living in a Chaotic World*

Hard Lessons - *Understanding and Addressing the Dangerous Challenges Facing Today's Youth*

Dr. Woodhouse is currently working on a book that focuses on the billion dollar "How to" industry and the obstacles it presents to authentic human growth and relationships.

For more information regarding Dr. Woodhouse, the reader can visit her web site at **www.laurenwoodhouse.com**

Suggested Reading

Anderson, E., "The Code of the Streets," *Hope Magazine*, Mar./Apr.1996.

Boca Raton News, June 14, 1998, editorial.

Campbell, A., *Men, Women and Aggression*, HarperCollins, 1993.

Calhoun, J., U.S. National Crime Prevention Council, Address to the International Crime Symposium, Vancouver, B.C. Apr., 1996.

Darden, C., *In Contempt*, HarperCollins, New York, 1996.

Klein, M. and Maxson, C., "Street Gang Violence," in *Violent Crime, Violent Criminals*, ed. N.Weiner, Sage Press, Newbury Park, 1998.

Lerner, H., *The Dance of Anger*, Harper and Row, New York, 1985.

Shaw, James, PhD, *Violence and Education*, doctoral thesis, UCLA, 1996.

Straus, M.A., Gelles, R.J. and Steinmetz, S., *Behind Closed Doors: Violence in the American Family*, Anchor Press, New York, 1998.

Whiskin, N., from "Crime Concern" – *Address to the International Crime Symposium*, Vancouver, B.C. Apr., 1996.

"Tougher Penalties for Youth Offenders," *The Ottawa Citizen*, 13/3/99.

Woodhouse, Lauren J., *Hard Lessons, Understanding and Addressing the Dangerous Challenges Facing Today's Youth*, CDG Books, Toronto, 2000.